Without Answers

*Studies in Ethics and the
Philosophy of Religion*

Without Answers

by

RUSH RHEES

SCHOCKEN BOOKS · NEW YORK

Published in U.S.A. in 1969
by Schocken Books Inc.
67 Park Avenue, New York, N.Y. 10016
Library of Congress Catalog Card No. 73-88218
© Rush Rhees 1969

Printed in Great Britain

Contents

Editorial Note

I have gathered these papers with the permission of Rush Rhees. They have been gathered from two sources: first, published and unpublished papers; and second, letters written to colleagues, students and friends on various occasions. There may well be letters by Rush Rhees which are just as important as those in this volume. I have made my selection from those I happened to know about. It does not follow that Rush Rhees himself would have selected the papers and letters I have chosen, or that he would have ordered them as I have done.

The first two papers are based on talks to first year students not reading philosophy. Numbers 3–5 are the only papers in the collection to be published previously. Numbers 3 and 4 were first published as a critical notice and article respectively in *Mind*, Vol. LVI, 1947. We are grateful to the Editor for permission to use the material here. Number 5 was first published in *Proceedings of the Aristotelian Society*, Supp. Vol. XXIII, 1949. We are grateful to the Editor for permission to use the material here. Numbers 6 and 14 are hitherto unpublished papers. With the exception of paper 14, numbers 7–17 are taken from letters written to various people between 1954 and 1966. Of these, numbers 7, 9 and 16 were written as notes on discussions in the Philosophical Society at the University College of Swansea. I am responsible for the titles of numbers 7, 9–12, 15 and 16. All other titles, including that of the collection, were provided by Rush Rhees, who also provided the Index. I am grateful to Mr. H. O. Mounce for helping me with the proof reading.

D. Z. PHILLIPS

Swansea, August 1968

1

A Scientific Age

The question is what science has done for the general outlook of our age.

This is not a question about the influence of machines and medicines. They have changed our outlook, certainly, and science has made that possible. But that is not the influence of science itself.

It might be said that science has brought a general enlightenment and a better understanding of things than other ages showed. But the idea of a general enlightenment is puzzling. We may need wisdom and understanding in most things—in business and in politics and in marriage, as well as in medicine and in the use of natural resources. But we may wonder whether it is the same wisdom in all; and whether that is anything that science could bring.

Scientific understanding is what scientists show in their own fields—in physics and in biology, for instance. There will never be very many scientists, and scientific understanding will never be a common thing. But science may influence our understanding of things in other ways—not by what it teaches us about them, but, or so it is said, by the way in which it teaches us to look at them. The scientific outlook, it is held, need not be confined to the special inquiries of science. It is largely a matter of adopting scientific methods in what we do. And a scientific age would treat all problems in that way.

That is not a scientific view, and I do not know how

many scientists hold it. But it is connected with the influence which science is having now. It suggests that the influence of science is chiefly in the spread of its methods and in the increasing trust in them. But those who welcome this also ascribe to the 'outlook' an influence which science might have in people's lives, though in a different way. And there is a confusion in this which makes it harder to see what is happening. The serious pursuit of science in any community may have an influence for the growth of culture and of understanding. But not by making men scientific or by making them think scientifically. It might be furthered if more could appreciate what scientific investigation is. But it is idle to hope that this will ever be widespread. And the idea that there is something scientific about adopting 'scientific methods' can only hinder it.

Even men of science have made claims for the 'outlook' latterly that are extravagant and shallow. So we find someone hoping for 'an ever increasing spread of the scientific outlook until it has become universal', when 'the human race will at last become adult, and the fairy tales of its infancy will be recognized for what they are'.[1]

To suggest that the spread of the scientific outlook will make the human race adult, seems to me itself a piece of childishness. If it is really meant that the human *race* has had an infancy and is to become adult, then I do not understand this, and I wonder what it means in science. But if it is meant that with the spread of the scientific outlook the human race will for the first time ('at last') become a race of adults, then I repeat that it is childish. As though our parents, or at any rate our grandparents, were less adult than we are. Or as though, perhaps, the men of earlier centuries were really less men than we are. And as though 'fairy tales' were all that had been lost in the transition. Compare our age with the Elizabethan age as regards vitality and variety of interests; or as regards initiative and adventure.

I do not believe that even scientists could talk that way if

[1] G. Burniston Brown, *Science, Its Method and Its Philosophy*, London, 1950. p. 181.

they had not fallen into thinking that there can be only one standard. The idea seems to be that so long as anything is not treated in a scientific way, it is being treated in an imperfect ('infantile') way. But reflexion would show dozens of cases where this is not so. When a doctor thinks over his examination of a patient, he may say something like, 'It seemed to me that he was not being entirely truthful in what he told me'. Here the doctor does not use anything like 'scientific method' or precise methods of measurement. And his work would not be improved if he tried to introduce them. Or again, to what extent can a judge be 'scientific' in his analysis and weighing of evidence? It may be urged that courts should accept the scientific evidence in the matter, say, of blood tests to determine paternity. But the judgment of the case, including very often a decision as to what is more important and what is less so, will be unlike the use of scientific measurements or tests, however widely we may introduce these to decide special issues of fact. There are many cases where the legal issue is not primarily one of fact at all, but rather of rights and claims. Here the judge has to weigh the different and conflicting interests that are involved, and decide which is of overriding importance. Such judgments—judgments concerning the liberty of the individual and the rights of the community, for instance—may affect our way of living more fundamentally than decisions on questions of fact ever can. And we may doubt if 'an ever increasing spread of the scientific outlook' will make them more enlightened than they were in former times. They will be *different*, no doubt, and the spread of the scientific outlook may help indirectly to make them so; but it does not make them more intelligent or more enlightened.

Or take education. What can be scientific about this? There may be any number of scientific 'aids' to education, but this does not mean that the work of educating itself is scientific, or that its problems can be solved by scientific methods. 'Classifying' children by any number of tests is not educating them. And even if we grant that the study of psychology may make a teacher wiser and more alive to various difficulties, the difference between a good teacher and a poor one is still not a matter of being more or less infused with the scientific outlook. Nor is there any reason to think that men in former ages must have been poor teachers if they disregarded it.

Industry is much more complicated, and I had better not try to speak of it in any general way. I think there have been serious misunderstandings of what science has done and can do here. But I will refer only to the special question of 'incentives'. There has been a good deal of study of this, but we have nothing like a science of it, and I doubt if we shall. This is partly because working—how you apply yourself to your work, and what it means in your life—is not a scientific business; just as little as enjoying yourself is. We are no nearer to a science of it when we make tests of 'aptitudes', or of 'fatigue' and so on; or even when we make experiments with different kinds of incentives in different factories. Those incentives relate generally to work of rather limited kinds—to repetitive and mechanical factory work— and we study how it may be influenced so as to improve the 'productivity' of the factory as a whole. If we confine ourselves to this, we leave out issues which are more fundamental: what the man's work means to him and to his life. We are concerned with palliatives or inducements of one kind or another; which leaves the fundamental matter where it was. This is not a stricture on such studies, provided they are not trusted with more than they can do. How we go to work is not something that can be discovered by scientific methods, and it cannot be scientifically controlled.

Yet it is 'how we go to work' that determines in large measure the character of the society and of the age in which we live. If there is a decline here (I cannot discuss the meaning of this now), the result will be more catastrophic than anything which the spread of the scientific outlook could redeem.

Or finally, consider friendship. Friendships may be imperfect, and perhaps infantile; or they may show maturity as nothing else can. There are difficulties and problems in friendship, and the growth of an adult outlook comes largely in connexion with them. But there can be no question of 'methods' here. In such difficulties, one is inclined to say, there can be no help, unless it is what also comes from friendship. Certainly the scientific outlook would be beside the point.

So we cannot say of all we do that it were better if it were done scientifically. Nor should we be more adult if we adopted a scientific outlook in these things. There may have been attempts and there will be more, to bring something which men call 'scientific method' into them. But this only shows how a preoccupation with the manners and achievements of science may help to make men stupid. The achievements of science have been enormous; but I do not think they have made men wiser—not the generality of men, at any rate. There is wisdom in science, but that is of another kind, as I shall try to show. There is no reason to think that the methods which have been successful in science will be of help in the face of other difficulties which are not scientific problems at all. If men think that scientific methods *must* help here, they generally ignore or falsify the difficulties. And the result can only be to weaken men's thinking in those questions that most concern them and their lives.

It may be felt that I have avoided the important issue here. All our experience with scientific methods, it may be said, has proved them the most reliable way of finding out about the world. It is only by keeping to scientific methods that we can hope to know what the world is really like. Otherwise we keep to fancies. And surely it is the part of wisdom to see this—to see the difference between a knowledge of the world and idle fancies about it. That does concern men's lives. It makes the deepest difference to them. The difference that there is between an adult and an infantile outlook.

Now it may be the part of wisdom to replace fancy by understanding. And perhaps there can be no true wisdom without trying to understand the world. But I do not think science can help us here. Science does tell us a great deal about 'the world around us'. It tells us about living things and chemical substances and stars; it tells us how the motions of bodies are influenced, how heat is radiated and so on. That is often what is meant, I suppose, when people say that science furnishes the surest method of finding out about the world. But that statement may suggest something else, which is a serious misunderstanding. It often suggests that science can provide an answer to questions with which it is really not concerned. In fact, of course, 'the world' is not a subject of scientific investigation. Heat is, and light is, and living organisms are; but not the world. When men are troubled to know what the world is like then in all conscience it is hard to know just what they are asking; and for the most part they could not say themselves. They want to understand the world; which, for one reason or another, they may feel they cannot understand. It is partly a question of understanding their own existence in the world, and of understanding what they are faced with. I do not think those two can be separated. Asking what the world is like, is never a purely theoretical question; though it is not in the ordinary sense a practical question either. If anyone does arrive at a view of the world, this generally makes a difference to his life, and a difference unlike any that comes from a better knowledge of facts (as it might make a difference to my life if I knew more about the weather). I do not think that science can give any such understanding of the world, or that it is in any way concerned to do so. That is why I do not think that scientific discoveries have made men wiser.

But the prevalence of science affects the way we think of things, or look at things, besides the special matters which it investigates. It may affect the way in which we understand questions in religion or in art, for instance, even if we are not trying to introduce scientific method into them. If anyone were to speak about religious doctrines now in the way in which he might have spoken in the thirteenth century, we should hardly listen to him. Not so much because he would be offering views which science has shown to be wrong, but because his whole way of arguing or presenting his case would seem unconvincing to us. It would not strike us as an argument at all—we might call it a verbal subterfuge —and we should not understand how anyone could be impressed by it. Consider the 'evidence' that was supposed to be afforded by miracles. The difficulty is not because science has shown that there can be no miracles. (How could it show that?) Our difficulty is partly in understanding what a miracle would *be*; and this is a result of our scientific ideas—a result of the mass of preconceptions from which we start and which we cannot escape, regarding how things should be viewed. And we find it even more difficult to see what could be meant by accepting a miracle as *evidence* for anything. For those who did accept them, they obviously had a force which we just cannot understand. And this is not because science has shown that they were *wrong* in finding such force in them. But the scientific treatment of natural events has come to take our attention and play a rôle in our lives as it never did for them. And we cannot move outside it in our thinking.

More recent changes in our ways of thinking would illustrate the same point. If we are looking for an explanation of someone's failings, the most convincing suggestion is generally that it was something that happened in his early childhood. This is not because we have tried explanations of other sorts. It is just that our minds move that way now.

In all this science has affected our view of things. But this is not a view of things which science has discovered for us, or which we have reached in any scientific way. We have come to rule out certain questions and certain sorts of explanations. Perhaps it is good that we have. But all this lies outside anything which scientific methods can decide.

Nor does this outlook do for our lives what the methods do for science. They may strengthen the spirit of inquiry there, as well as directing it. The scientific outlook does neither; not as it operates outside science, anyway. Perhaps it removes idle fancies. It does not bring a spirit of scientific curiosity and investigation.

I said earlier that there may be wisdom in science, but that it brings confusions if we think that its results reveal to us what the world is like. Perhaps the most serious of these is what I may call a confusion about profundity. If the discoveries of science really did show us what the world is like, they would be profoundly important in a way that has nothing to do with the health and happiness of mankind. They do not do that. And the illusion that they do has helped men to lose their sense of profundity and to confuse it with what is sham.

It is not hard to see that profundity may be confused with what is complicated or esoteric. And I dare say some people make this mistake when they think of science as profound: it is 'beyond us', so it must be deep. (You might as well suppose that what he says is profound if he says it in Latin.) It is easy to think there is something deep in anything that is very impressive. And it is especially common to confuse profundity with what is awesome or overpowering. What astronomers tell us may seem profound, because the endless spaces, the huge numbers and the incredible ages make us gasp. There are also other reasons why people think there is something profound to be learned here, but I think they all show a fundamental misconception. For I think it is nonsense to suppose that there can ever be a profound discovery.

What is deep need not be obscure. For instance, the reply of Jesus when asked about the woman taken in adultery was deep; it was not obscure.

There is profundity in science. It has to do with the problems that are raised and the way in which they are treated. In physics, for instance, the treatment of a problem may also be the development of a view as to what physical investigation is concerned with, or what sort of answers physics must try to give. Newton's work was deep, partly through his conception of the general problem of explaining physical phenomena in terms of motion and mass. Today we might question that. We might say that the fundamental character of physics cannot lie in the study of motion as he

..

conceived it. This would be to raise again the deepest question that Newton raised and answered. If the answer is different now, this does not mean that Newton's work is less profound.

Something similar could be said of the work of Maxwell, I suppose, and of others. Of Carnot and of Mayer; and perhaps of Einstein.

It is easy to misunderstand this. It does not mean that a discussion of what physics is would be more profound than physics itself. That would be irrelevant anyway. There have been inquiries into 'the nature of physical knowledge' which were not investigations in physics, even if physicists took part in them. And if such inquiries were profound, that would not mean that physics was. Newton may have said profound things about physics, but they were part of a deep treatment of the subject; of a profound scientific investigation.

If we emphasize especially the character of the investigation, this must not suggest that what it is about does not matter. The sincerity and earnestness of an investigation would obviously not make it deep. That can come only from what is treated, from the depth of the problems. But these are the problems that cannot be recognized apart from the investigation to which they belong. If someone should say, 'Physics deals with profound questions, such as the nature of the stellar universe and the nature of matter and of energy'—this would be misleading. There need not be anything deep in the treatment of such questions, or in the questions themselves. On the other hand there may be. Physics may be profound. The stars are not; neither are atoms. And learning the truth about the stars, or learning the truth about matter, need have nothing profound in it. Newton's work was not deep because of what he showed about the mechanics of the solar system, or because his conclusions relate to all bodies in all space. In studying such questions Newton was concerned with deep problems. But what makes the problems deep is not the objects they treat

2—WA •

of. That would be like confusing depth with what is esoteric or what is vast.

The deep problems which a scientist may recognize are problems of his science, and they do not stand by themselves. The depth of what he has said about them does not depend so much on whether his answers can be accepted just as they were given. In one sense it does not matter whether they were right or wrong. Of course the scientist's work could not be deep if he were indifferent to that himself. It would not be serious investigation at all. But the profundity of his work lies rather in his perception of what sort of answers they are.

From a serious investigation we may gain some sense of what is at issue there. And the profundity of the problem lies at least to some extent in that. What is at issue is not just the answer to a particular problem, though it is not something separate from it. What is at issue is the understanding that is sought in science. This cannot be described independently of the work of the sciences themselves. Science is not carried on to decide something else. But what is at issue in the work of physicists may be physics—may be the sort of inquiry that there can be in such matters. Ideas have changed regarding what the most fundamental questions are, and regarding the fundamental character of the investigation. To see that the older and the more recent conceptions are in an important way concerned with the same thing, would be to see that they have been concerned with understanding, as I would speak of it here; not in the sense in which physicists may be concerned with understanding the problems of a particular field, such as the propagation of light, for instance, but as they are concerned with the sort of understanding or investigation that physics is or can be. To say that this is what is at issue, would mean perhaps that physics is not just taken for granted; and that it depends on the way the problems are solved. The sense of their importance may lie in that, and the profound way in which they are treated may lie there also.

This does not mean that physics is 'just thinking'. But

neither is experiment just testing. Experiments are important because they *are* physical investigation. Experiments may be done in 'research' of various kinds, perhaps in connexion with some branch of industry, when the scientist may be working on problems to which he has been assigned. Such experiments may be of high quality. But I imagine that the work generally does not have the same character as experimental physics. And if it does, that is because of its bearing on physics, and not because of its success in finding what was asked by industry. It is in physics, and as the development of physical investigation, that experimental work may be deep. And there can be nothing deep in physics without it. Of course we should not say that scientists find their answers by 'deep thinking'—unless we should call the devising of the experiments deep thinking. And what may be deep in that is just what is deep in physical investigation anyway. What is at issue in the experiment then is not merely whether the outcome will be of this sort or another. The result of the experiment may be profoundly important. If it is, this is an importance for physics and for all that physics is trying to do.

I have tried to emphasize the confusion of saying that the discoveries of science show us what the world is like; or that 'the scientific method' is a way of finding out about the world. 'Science is what scientists do.' Science as it was carried on by Newton, Maxwell and others, *does* show us something about the world. And its latest discoveries do not show us more.[1]

---

[1] A man may learn about the stars or the structure of the earth, and be no wiser. If he learns this without an understanding of the sort of problems that disturb astronomers or geologists, he may only be more stupid. Cf. Molière, *Les Femmes Savantes*, Acte IV, Scène III:

Trissotin
J'ai cru jusques ici que c'étoit l'ignorance
Qui faisoit les grands sots, et non pas la science.

Citandere
Vous avez cru fort mal, et je vous suis garant
Qu'un sot savant est sot plus qu'un sot ignorant.

We may say that Newton's work was deep, and we may say that the work of Michaelangelo was deep. Obviously there are wide differences, and we do not mean quite the same in each case. But they have something in common. The profundity of Newton's work appears both in the problems that it raises and also in the power of the treatment. And if we take for instance Michaelangelo's picture of the creation of Adam in the Sistine Chapel, we see how depth and strength are almost one and the same—the power of his treatment (the raiment of God, for example) is what gives it the depth that it has. Here is a matter that can be treated only with energy or not at all: but with energy that is also profound. Think of any treatment in which there might have been decoration and splendour—which could have nothing to do with the problem that creation is.

No doubt there is no 'problem' as something to be solved. We could hardly distinguish between Michaelangelo's conception of the problem and his answer to it.

This is not the profundity of science. Michaelangelo's picture is not an investigation, and it is not a discussion of the matters which it treats. They can hardly be discussed anyway, and perhaps they can be treated only in painting. At any rate they are unlike anything that is the concern of science. But the depth of the picture does go with a search for understanding and with a deep sense of what is at issue in that. The sense of this is not something separate but is seen in the way in which the different matters are treated in the entire conception. And in this I think there are analogies to what may be deep in scientific investigation. What it shows about the world—is certainly not a picture of the world. But it is not symbolism either. It shows what it does because it is as deep as it is. This does not mean that when we appreciate the depth we appreciate something 'beyond' the picture rather than what is there. Much the same is true in science. The profundity that we may recognize in a work in physics is not something that we could see except by seeing the great science that is there. But the work shows us something about the world by being the profound investigation that it is. It is by this that we may see things differently and have a deeper sense of what is at issue.[1]

[1] People generally avoid discussions of profundity, because depth is not achieved by talking about it, and the effort to be profound yields only bathos. In this discussion I do not try to show anyone what profundity is. I know that it can be seen only where it is found. My business is with confusions concerning it: and those especially which join opinions of what we may expect from science.

2

Science and Questioning

Someone says, 'I will oppose anything which limits or hampers the pursuit of science'.

And I admire this.

But if he says, 'I will do so because of the great importance of science for mankind'—things have become confused.

Suppose I asked someone 'Why is physics important?' and for answer he told me what physicists do (what the study of physics is).

Either you go in for science, or you don't. Either you are interested in science, or you're not.

But people have given a false generality to science; as though science said clearly and fully what everyone has been fumbling after all along; as though anything we say would be more accurately expressed in scientific terms. Or perhaps, that science gets to the bed rock of all our beliefs. So when we distinguish science from our everyday observations and descriptions of things, this is a distinction in levels or grades of accuracy, rather than in subject matter. This is suggesting that the various results in physics or in biology have a universal application which in fact they do not have. It seems almost as though there were some difficulty in recognizing that the sciences are these special forms of investigation, in which some people spend their lives, alongside all the people who are doing other things.

The confusion may appear when people speak of enlightenment. For it seems as though some would argue: since scientists know more than scientists did 150 years ago, therefore we are more enlightened than people were then. In other words, the progress of science must also have been—though perhaps on a different level—a progress for everyone in the society.

But if we, who are not scientists, are more enlightened now, this is not a scientific enlightenment—it has not come from science, as understanding comes from a scientific explanation to one who can follow it. If we say that the growth of science has made us more enlightened, it is not clear *how* science is responsible. And it cannot be clear, unless 'more enlightened' can be made definite.

It is often said that science has freed us from superstitions. There are superstitions among us, often enough—when we are backing race-horses, for instance. The growth of science has not discouraged this, and probably never will. But it may be said that we're less superstitious towards natural obstacles and disasters. We are prepared to study the obstacles we meet: we ask what would be needed to remove them, or we ask to what extent our plans must be changed or adjusted in face of them. This is a common reaction to human diseases, failures of crops, scarcity of fuel, etc. We have a rough idea of the sorts of explanations such things have had. We can think of possibilities and remedies which would not have occurred to people three centuries ago. More and more we can see a scientific spirit in the way we react to obstacles—instead of capitulating or running away from them. And this may seem like the difference between a mature and an infantile attitude.

But even if the analogy were stronger—and even if people generally did take their troubles in a scientific spirit now—we could not argue that we are more mature than the people of the seventeenth century were. We may have explanations and remedies for a wider range of natural happenings. A second year undergraduate in physics will probably know laws and methods which Newton did not know—

but we do not conclude that he is a more intelligent scientist than Newton was. The maturity of our time is nothing to notice. A man who goes to the doctor with his pains is not more mature than he would be in bearing them when they were incurable. An illiterate peasant may be more mature, less infantile in face of trouble, than an accomplished scientist.

The present undergraduate cannot understand the problems and difficulties Newton was facing; nor estimate what it would take to solve them in seventeenth century physics. Neither can we guess what the practical problems and difficulties of the people of that time were. We cannot weigh their difficulties with ours. And we cannot say how we'd react in their place.

When we speak of a progressive enlightenment, we take for granted a common measure where we cannot even imagine one.

Suppose it were said that science has freed us from subjection to fate. And suppose we asked *how* science has done this.

As though men had spoken of fate because they knew no better. As though the reasoned beliefs of science could *replace* any thought of fate.

Wittgenstein spoke of the difference between a man who when a disaster happens, asks: 'Who was responsible for this?', and the man who says 'It is the will of God' or 'It is fate'. 'It is fate' is not meant to answer the question 'Who is responsible?' The man who says it does not ask that question.

There may be a scientific explanation of what has happened; but then 'explaining what has happened' is ambiguous. Suppose there has been an earthquake, and geologists now give an explanation of it. This will not be an answer to the woman who has lost her home and her child and asks 'Why?' It does not make it easier to understand 'what has befallen us'. And the woman's question, though it may drive her mad, does not seek an answer. 'It was fate' may some day come to take the place of asking.

A man whose son is in danger of death may say, 'The outcome will be whatever is fated to be'. And he is not predicting anything. Or if he says, 'Whatever happens will be the will of God'—this cannot *mislead* us about what is going to happen.

Horoscopes may mislead people sometimes (I do not know). Perhaps a fortune teller sometimes does. And we'd call a man deluded if he thought a spell had been cast on him compelling him to sell his farm, against the interests of himself and his family. But when I'm misled like this I am given to believe that this particular event will happen in my life, or that this particular danger will threaten me at such and such a time. There is no such prediction when the man I mentioned earlier says, 'Whatever happens, it will be as fate has ordered'.

If someone took a fortune teller's warnings so to heart that he changed important decisions and gave up important projects, we might call him stupid, and if he were my friend I should try to get him to see reason; though I do not know how I should go about it. I imagine that people before the rise of modern science would have judged the man much as we do. They probably had as good an idea as we of what might work in bringing him away from this credulity. Or are there scientific techniques which would make us more competent?

We may think of 'fatalism' as a conviction that we can do nothing about it—without even trying to investigate to see what could be done. We are familiar enough with this at the present time, and I wonder if the growth of science has made it less common than it was. People then deplored it, as we do. And we use their language in trying to jolt our friends out of it. We quote Shakespeare too often: 'The fault, dear Brutus, lies not in our stars, but in ourselves, that we are underlings'. This may not be effective, and probably it was not then. But I wonder if we have more resources for this than they did. A defeatist fatalism could no more be cured by scientific methods than scientific reasonings could make a man courageous.

(Our scientists spend much of their public statements in warning us against *risks*. If a man is timid, the study of science may make him more so.)

'We can be masters of our destinies' amounts to: 'Don't imagine that there's nothing you can do'. If we read that 'Science can make us masters of our destinies', this is also a slogan but the sense is less plain. Part of it is, that we should not think we are playthings of forces we cannot understand.

This misunderstands the notion of 'forces' that would be meant if we said that. If a man says 'It was nobody's fault; it had to be', this is not the necessity expressed in the laws of mechanics. And if he says we are the playthings of forces we cannot understand, he is thinking of what happens in human affairs, not the forces a physicist measures and calculates. 'We *can* understand the forces to which we are subject' would mean we can understand the physical forces; and this is not challenged.

When we think of our lives, or the people we know or the histories we read, we see coincidence and accident.

In this sense, accident is something we cannot prevent.

It may be contrasted with what makes sense, what has a point in connexion with what happened before—or what can be understood in connexion with what is happening and has happened.

It is connected also with ideas of destiny or of fate. And then it can be seen as characteristic of 'existence in space and time'. People are born where they are—in these places, at these times and in these circumstances. What anyone learns, what he can aspire to, the friends and the teachers that he finds ... is limited by where he is, what he can reach and when he is living. And the fact that I cannot redress the worst wrongs I have done is connected with this as well. If I asked 'Why should those men have lived there and in those times, and I be living now and in this place?', there could be no answer.

The distribution of human beings has no more sense than the course of history does.

We speak of accepting fate. Or accepting the will of God. This means especially: accepting death. To talk of being 'masters' here would be nonsense.

II

People ask 'Why?' or 'What's happening?' It is foolish to think there must be a way of finding the answer. That would keep one from seeing what the question is—what difficulty it expresses.

It would be meaningless to speak of this sort of difficulty in science.

Yet it is important for the work of science that there are these questions.

Science is something that those who come to it now have inherited. They start with the particular science as it is now: what the mass of experiments and theories over centuries have made it; working with methods and equipment which are themselves applications of new discoveries. But the work of older scientists is important to them in other ways than just for its results.

When someone understands physics, it is not simply that he's mastered the techniques and can follow them. He understands the point of that investigation. He has acquired a nose for what is real or interesting physics and what is not. He has this from his own work in the field, and also from working together with others and from reading the works of scientists in other countries. This is related to what is sometimes called the 'background' of experimental science. A chemist or physicist takes it for granted that these and these circumstances may be relevant to the experiment, and others obviously are not. In an experiment on heat conductivity he will not wonder whether the colour of the curtains might make a difference. If you asked him *why* he disregards such things, he would think you were silly. This background is part of what he inherits. And anyone who questioned it would show that he did not know what was going on.

Perhaps most of pseudo-science is based on ignorance—especially ignorance of how scientists use the methods which they teach and describe. The publication of a startling theory may show that the author has misunderstood what physicists mean by the 'repeatability' of an experiment, for instance. Or the work may depend on a misuse of probability theory, or in some way try to build on incongruous calculations. And yet a work could show similar faults and not be pseudo-science: depending on the rôle the mistakes played in it. If we asked why this man's work, with so many blunders, is not called pseudo-science, when that other work is—the answer might vary from one case to another. There is no *general* answer to 'What is the difference between science and pseudo-science?'—any more than there is to 'What is science?' A formal logician will sometimes devise a 'mechanical method' for deciding the validity or consistency of certain sorts of complex expressions or transformations. But if we thought of devising such a method to determine the scientific or unscientific character of reports and theories, this itself would show a misunderstanding of what science is.

Science is what scientists do. There is no rule by which the form and range of this could be worked out here and now. Just as there is no rule by which a physicist or astronomer can know if extrapolation is justified in these circumstances. Wild extrapolations may be a recognized danger. But if we asked a scientist 'How do you know when it is *not* wild?' he might answer, 'Well, you just do'.

Since special scientists develop a nose for what is sound or important in their fields, we might think they would be better qualified than most to tell pseudo-science from what is genuine in other fields as well. Probably some are, but not all. Sometimes the special training seems to have given a scientist a penchant for what *looks* like science—perhaps in certain social questions—hardly asking if the subject can be treated in this way. Or a scientist makes proposals in a way that he would never countenance in his own field. A physicist who has become aware of some elementary relations between money and credit, may produce books and pamphlets advocating a special theory in economics, apparently basing his economics on an account of energy in physics and in physiology: and all with the fervour of a perpetual motion fanatic. Or again, a physicist, with a Nobel Prize for his work in connexion with transistors, puts forward in public lectures a combination of racial theories, genetics and social planning, complaining that 'inverted liberals' are preventing research into the subject. A man may hold these views; but if he said they were the outcome of scientific thinking ('research'), I guess this would be sham—although it might be said in good faith. And these are not unusual examples.

I have said that those who study science learn more from their teachers than methods and results. What is it that those have learned who see that in excursions like these the scientific spirit has perished? We cannot say that they have learned more physics. It may be just that they still take questions seriously even when they have left the forms of physical experiment and measurement. And in pseudo-science the respect for questions is lost: the abuse of method is pseudo-science when it is no longer *investigation*, but pretends to be.

This spirit or sense of questions may be quickened, I think, when scientists are alive to questions that are not part of science.

In physics people ask questions. Their phraseology has its meaning in the special work they do, and means nothing to those who have done no physics. But this phraseology has grown among people speaking as they also speak with people not doing physics. It was through the ordinary ways of speaking that they recognized the need for special terms and special symbolism and syntax. Otherwise they would not be terms and syntax, but just empty gestures and scribbles. To say that the symbolism and syntax of physics is a 'development' of ordinary language would be misleading. But unless things were said and questions asked outside physics, there would not be physics.

The language I speak is kept alive and kept natural by people, mostly, to whom I never speak or listen (whom I never see). Phrases and expressions are in the air and form the natural way of speaking, theirs and mine. People speak with one another at work and relaxing and at home, and they are troubled by questions that are no concern of science. It would be a death wish for science to hope that some day all speech and all questions might be scientific.

3

Philosophy and Science

Cornforth thinks that 'the advance of science provides the means for the solution of the problems of philosophy' (p. 263).[1] He thinks Bacon, Hobbes and, in a measure, Locke recognized this. Berkeley, Hume, Kant, Mach, Russell, Wittgenstein and Carnap have been chiefly concerned with trying to deny it. And this effort 'reflects' the wishes of the capitalist class that it should be denied. For the view that science provides the means for solving the problems of philosophy is a revolutionary view (even if Bacon held it). And, of course, to deny it is 'reactionary'.

But the view leads Cornforth to misconceive the problems and discussions he refers to. He thinks the philosophies he criticizes deny 'the independent existence of the objective material world'. (Russell, Wittgenstein and Carnap differ from Berkeley only in that their denial of it is underhanded and tricky.) They are all forms of subjectivism. And he thinks that science provides the refutation of subjectivism, because science shows that the world exists independently. Cornforth never explains or discusses the phrase 'exists independently'. He often writes 'exists independently of any consciousness', and he uses 'exists outside consciousness' as equivalent. But the sense is still obscure.

[1] *Science versus Idealism: An Examination of 'Pure Empiricism' and Modern Logic*, By Maurice Cornforth (London: Lawrence and Wishart, 1946). Mr. Cornforth no longer holds the views on the relations of science and philosophy put forward in this book.

And in arguing that science gives proof of the independent existence of matter or material things he misunderstands what the idealists or subjectivists were saying. The question whether material things exist independently, as it arose in discussions like Berkeley's, is not a question of science. And it was not by ignoring the results of science that idealists were led to their position. Nor can the issue be settled by anything like a scientific investigation.

It might be said that what I perceive or what I think about exists independently, because it may exist when I do not perceive it and am not thinking of it.

But a statement such as 'These stones will exist when they are not thought about' would be unusual, and it might not be clear just what was being said. It looks almost like a prediction; as though you were saying something about these stones in particular. And so it may seem like saying, for instance, 'These stones will still be here after I am dead'. But that is not what I want to say when I say they exist independently. For a soap bubble and a whiff of steam exist independently as much as the stones do. I am not really saying anything *about* the stones, anyway. It is not as though the stones were different in some respect from anything else.

When would you ask such a question as, 'Will these things exist when they are not thought about?' And what would you want to know? What sort of investigation might help you to answer it? It is clearly not a question you would ask about any physical object. And you would not ask it about a mental image or an impression either. If you asked it at all, I suppose it would be because you wondered whether you were just having an image or whether you were seeing a real thing. And you would try to settle the question by asking other people, changing your position, seeing whether you could touch it and so on, and not by trying to see whether it really does exist when it is not thought about.

So it is a question whether these are real things— whether they are physical objects. But if you say that phys-ical objects exist when no one is thinking of them, you are not saying what physical objects are like. You are not ascribing any 'power' to them. It is not like saying that they are impervious to something or other. And it is not as though physical objects would be different in nature if that were not so—in the sense that it would make any difference to what you observe or what you can do with them.

It may be said that you have to assume their uninterrupted existence in order to account for their present condition, or in order to account for changes from what was observed earlier. And you *have* to assume this and you *have* to account for this because you are talking about physical objects. If it is an image, you do not have to account for its appearance in that way. And it is not really an assumption in the ordinary sense. It is not like assuming that the body must have been dead for so long in order to account for its present condition. The point is rather that any special assumption you do make in order to account for the present condition of these objects is an assumption of a particular form, or within a particular grammar. If you say that you have to account for their present condition in such and such ways, then this *is* 'assuming' their continued existence. And I put 'assuming' in inverted commas, because that is not really an assumption which you put forward or try to test at all. It would be better to say that it describes the kind of 'accounting for things' that goes on in such cases.

'My house has existed while I have been asleep.' 'How do you know?' 'Because it has not been destroyed.' (The question 'How do you know?' makes a difference, apparently.) What would make the bother, and upset our understanding, would be the interruption of certain constant sorts of behaviour. 'Continued existence' is a feature of the descriptions we give of things, of the properties we assign to them; or rather, it has to do with what is meant by 'assigning properties' in such cases. It is not itself a property, or anything we conclude from their behaviours. Assigning properties to things—describing things—is different from assigning properties to images or impressions. (For one thing, you do not investigate to see whether the image really has that property.) And the difference here is one of grammar—of what difference it makes to say one thing or another.

'Is the difference between real things and images only a difference in the way you speak about them, then? And could you change about and use the physical object grammar in what you say about images?'

That would be mistaking images for physical objects (which is not like mistaking a wax-work for a man).

Of course, the difference between images and physical objects is not a difference of words. But if you say it is a difference of nature—then I suppose we might ask, what *sort* of difference of nature. If we said there was a difference in the nature of iron and copper, we could say what the difference is by specifying the properties of the one that are not found in the other. But that is not what the difference between the image of a flower and a real flower is like. You may 'carry out tests' to see whether it is a real flower or just an image. But the difference here, we might say, is in the 'see whether'. For it is not an investigation to see whether it has certain properties or not.

You could not say, for instance, that one difference is that the image will not grow or will not attract bees. Or if you did, this would be confused and misleading. It would apply to paper flowers, for instance. And any difference of that sort is one that might hold between physical objects. (Even if you can put your finger through it, it might conceivably be a flower shape of coloured smoke or coloured light.) In fact, if you put the difference in that way it could *only* hold between physical objects.

What such 'tests' do is not to bring out the differences between real things and images. And if you decide, 'It's only an image', this is not like deciding 'It's only paper'. It is not in the same way a conclusion you draw about it from your investigations. Perhaps you can say they change your way of looking at it. You will not ask the same sort of questions about it, at any rate ('How did it get there?', etc.). (If you called the investigation 'testing an hypothesis', would it be an hypothesis about what you saw or about yourself? Or neither?)

You can say that the difference between images and things is a difference in 'mode of existence', if that makes anything clearer. The trouble is that 'mode of existence' is likely to be taken for something like 'mode of operation', and then the tendency is to treat images like a class of physical objects with a special mode of operation, which obscures the whole difference.

And there are special difficulties about such a phrase as *'independent* existence', or about saying that impressions or images do not exist independently. This is partly because the reference is to a dependence on *consciousness*; and it is hard to see what sort of dependence that could be, or how it could be recognised. It is clearly not a causal dependence, anyway. If you say that images cannot exist without consciousness of them, this is not like saying that sounds cannot exist in a vacuum; the 'cannot' is obviously different. That is why it makes no sense to try to show or discover the 'dependence'.[1] It is the same when it is said that images exist only 'in the mind' and physical objects are 'outside'.

What 'subjectivists' do is to misunderstand what talking about physical objects is, and how this is different from talking about images or about impressions. But those who talk about the 'independent existence' or 'external existence' of physical objects are not clear about this difference either.

Cornforth, at any rate, shares most of the subjectivist confusions himself. And he is unable to show what is wrong with the theories he criticizes even when he has partly understood them. The objects of sense, he says, are 'contents of consciousness'. And the ideas of science are also contents of consciousness. The contents of consciousness do

---

[1] And for different reasons you cannot show a causal dependence on brain processes either. You cannot show that every time I have an image something happens in my brain, or that there is a change in my brain for every change in the image. But if you could, this would not show a difference between images and physical objects. It would suggest that images *were* physical objects.

not exist independently because they are 'parts' or 'aspects' or 'functions' (he does not say finally which, and perhaps it does not matter) of brain processes, and have no existence apart from the brain (p. 90). But they are 'conscious representations' of material things 'outside' consciousness. Material things themselves are never contents of consciousness, but are what the contents of consciousness refer to. 'The content of consciousness reflects reality, but reflects it in its own way, according to its own laws, and not with an exact correspondence' (p. 218). But science makes the correspondence more and more exact, and so gives us a more and more accurate 'picture of reality'. We might ask how we can know that the picture which science gives is a more accurate representation than what we had before; and Cornforth's answer is that the test is 'practice'—the fact that we can use the ideas of science to produce things in accordance with them. That is the 'test of the validity of knowledge' (p. 83). So material things are not mysterious or something we know not what, because science tells us so much about them, and because science enables us to produce such things ourselves.

He thinks the use of scientific knowledge to produce things is a refutation of subjectivism. But subjectivism is further refuted, he says, because it is 'in hopeless contradiction with what we know to be the case as a result of scientific investigations' (p. 93), and especially with the results of neurology and with the theory of evolution.

But such refutations ignore the problems, and mistake what the subjectivists or 'pure empiricists' were saying. Cornforth thinks that Berkeley and Kant and Mach all 'asserted that the external objective material world, the system of material processes which in their interaction with our own organic bodies produce sensations, is a meaningless supposition, without any grounds in experience or reason, mysterious, incomprehensible, absurd—in a word "metaphysical" ' (p. 80). He supports Engels's statement that 'in Kant's time our knowledge of natural objects was indeed so fragmentary that he might well suspect, behind the little we knew about each of them, a mysterious thing in itself. But one after another these ungraspable things have been grasped, analysed, and what is more, produced by the giant progress of science; and what we can produce, we certainly cannnot consider unknowable.' And Cornforth says in his own words that 'when we learn to produce it, the mysterious becomes comprehensible, the unknown becomes known, the "thing in itself" becomes a "thing for us" ' (p. 83). But what is mysterious and baffling in the question of what things are in themselves does not come from any scantiness of scientific knowledge; nor did that have anything to do with Kant's argument. For Kant the idea of producing a thing in itself would have been absurd; and however much we may learn about phenomena by producing them, they are still phenomena. This view may be untenable. But to suggest that Kant's difficulty is removed by the progress of science is just to ignore the difficulty.

Incidentally, for all Cornforth's assertions about the independent existence of the material world, his own view leaves the material world as mysterious and unknowable as ever things in themselves were for Kant. For on his view the progress of science can present us only with further contents of consciousness or further 'representations', and never with what is represented. He does not show how we could ever arrive at anything to be contrasted with 'contents of consciousness', or what would be meant by that. And the reference to 'practice' is no help. Whatever we may produce according to our ideas, we never see any result except new contents and new ideas. And if you say these 'refer' to something 'outside' or 'beyond' them, this reference is as mysterious after 'practice' as it was before. This is Berkeley's criticism of the theory of material substance, and it holds against any theory which tries to put the difference between things and impressions in the way Cornforth does.

Cornforth argues further that science has shown that material things exist independently of consciousness, since it has shown that all thought and all consciousness depends on the brain (pp. 92, 93). It follows that the brain does not depend on consciousness, but exists independently. This is argued especially in refutation of Mach's statement that 'bodies do not produce sensations, but complexes of elements (complexes of sensations) make up bodies'. Since the existence of sensations depends on the brain, the existence of the brain cannot depend on sensations. Therefore the brain is not a complex of sensations. So the view that bodies are complexes of sensations is refuted by science.

But such an argument can be made plausible only by the vagueness and ambiguity of 'depends on', together with a misunderstanding of Mach's[1] meaning when he said bodies were 'complexes of sensations'. Obviously Mach did not mean that a brain is a complex of sensations and not a complex of nerve fibres and cells. But suppose I look at a brain, and then say that what I see (and perhaps touch and smell) exists when I do not see it. The phenomenalist's puzzle is regarding the 'what I see'. He would argue that there are changes in what I see even when I am still looking at the brain—when I change my view point, shine a strong light on it, heat it and so on. The brain is supposed to be the same—the same body—throughout such changes. But what *is* it that is the same here, then? Mach said that all these various appearances, or 'sinnliche Elemente', are so connected with one another that if you return to the same position, illumination, temperature, you have the same appearace again. It is this *connexion* among sensible elements which constitutes the body. 'If we could measure all the sensible elements, we should say that the body consists in the satisfaction of certain *equations* which hold between the sensible elements.'[2] Whatever may be said against this view, it does not conflict with any account of the structure of the brain in terms of nerve fibres. And it is not a statement that the brain depends upon the existence of sensation in the way in which it depends on the existence of nerve

---

[1] Cornforth introduces Mach as a 'neo-Kantian', I suppose because Lenin does so. He describes the neo-Kantian movement as 'the movement which went backwards from Kant to pure empiricism'.

[2] *Prinzipien der Wärmelehre*, Leipzig, 1900, p. 424.

fibres. Nor does it prevent one from saying that I could not have sensations if I did not have a brain. 'There is a brain within my skull' does not mean that anyone is *having* sensations of it, on Mach's view; and still less that *I* am.

All this has to do with Mach's analysis of the conception of material substance as it appears in what he calls 'naïve understanding'. Mach tries to show how this is carried over into the conceptions of material substance that have appeared in various branches of scientific investigation— mechanics, the theory of heat and so on. Cornforth does not do this, because he does not seem to have thought much about science, or to have learned what Mach's writings might have taught him about it. But even in the naïve conception there are difficulties which Mach was concerned with and which Cornforth never faces—difficulties in speaking of something 'outside' or 'beyond' or 'behind' sensible appearances which 'produces' them. And they are not met by pointing to the discoveries of science, in physiology or anywhere else.

I think Mach was mistaken in what he said about sensible appearances. When I talk about the colour I see or the texture I feel, I am not talking about my impressions. But it is not easy to show this. And Cornforth does not attempt to.

Nor do you refute phenomenalism if you say that science has shown that there were material bodies before there were living things. The phenomenalist need not hold that if there were stones at that time, there must have been sense data at that time, any more than he need hold that if there are stones in that field now there must be sense data in that field now. And the former proposition is not really harder or more crucial for phenomenalism than the latter. Certainly, if you are talking about conditions in which no observations *could* have been made, the phenomenalist may wonder if it is clear what you are talking about. But if you say that what existed was something like what can be observed now, directly or indirectly (as when we measure high temperatures, for instance), the phenomenalist would say you have still to give an account of it in terms of the sort of observations that could have been made. The question of how or whether human beings could have got into positions to make just those observations at those times is not really relevant to the phenomenalist analysis, I think. If there are difficulties, they apply to the phenomenalist interpretation of *any* statement about what is not immediately observed; or, it may be argued, even to any statement about what *is* immediately observed. The particular conclusions of science do not change the issues. And it is absurd to say they prove the independent existence of matter—as if that were really something like proving the prehistoric existence of matter or of material things.

The obscurity of Cornforth's references to 'matter' appears also in what he says about 'the world' or 'Reality' or 'being' (he generally uses these expressions interchangeably). He thinks that idealism presents a false picture of the world, and one that is in conflict with the 'ever developing and ever more unified picture of the world' that is furnished by science. Science not only shows what the world is like, but it also provides an explanation of the world (p.242, and elsewhere). And it shows us our place and our destiny in it. (It shows us our destiny by showing us how we may be masters of our destiny.) The task of philosophy is to explain the significance of science; and this consists in making it clear that science *does* provide a picture of the world. That is what idealism denies; and this is why idealism is a false and perverted philosophy. The significance of the particular discoveries of science lies in their contribution to this world picture, or their contribution to the understanding of the nature of the world or of reality. That is Cornforth's view.

Now it might be said that science shows us certain techniques of investigation, and it shows us the results of particular investigations and experiments. But it is not clear what would be meant by speaking of *the* significance of these investigations and these results. I suppose they might have a different significance according as you were interested in different sorts of application or in the development of theories. And it is not clear *what* significance you would bring out if you said they showed us something about the world. If you say, for instance, that thermodynamics shows us something about the world—what have you added to the particular statements of thermodynamics?

The idea seems to be that the development of thermodynamics, or any new scientific development, is a 'victory for science', and strengthens the view that science is the only way of arriving at truth. But what would it mean to say that science is a 'way of arriving at truth'? There are methods of distinguishing between true and false views and between true and false predictions in any science. But to say that science altogether is a method of arriving at truth would mean little. As though 'science' were a single and systematic inquiry, perhaps. I suppose the idea of a 'unified world picture' is intended to support such a view. But one difficulty would be in knowing just what science as a whole is trying to find out; as though there could be scientific investigation with no specific problem. And it is no help here to say that it is 'the nature of the world' or 'the nature of reality' that science is trying to discover.

In philosophy, people have asked about 'the nature of reality' or 'the nature of existence', and not always in the same way. Sometimes it has been a question of 'the general conditions of existence', and the inquiry into these has been part of an inquiry into 'the conditions of the possibility of discourse'. Perhaps the question 'How is experience possible?' is something similar. But these are not empirical conditions of existence, in the sense that they might be discovered experimentally (like the conditions of the existence of vegetation). They are conditions of intelligibility, or of what can be thought or spoken about.

If it is said that the progress of science reveals the nature of reality, this might mean that reality is shown to 'accord with' certain principles of scientific inquiry, such as determinism or the uniformity of nature. But these principles are not scientific laws, and they are not scientifically established. They do not describe anything that is itself an object of scientific investigation. And you cannot say that science shows that the world accords with them in the sense in which it shows that the processes of respiration accord with a certain theory of respiration. There is no scientific 'theory of reality'.

Cornforth speaks of a 'view of the nature of the world which science gives us grounds for accepting', in contrast to metaphysical views of the world like those of logical atomism. He thinks that science supports the view that the world consists of 'processes which interpenetrate and modify one another', and that 'the most general characteristic of reality is change and movement' (p. 137). So that science refutes the view that the world consists of simple substances.

But here there is a confusion about the use of such expressions as 'permanence' and 'change', or 'states' and 'processes'. If you said 'Science shows that everything changes' or 'Science shows that nothing is permanent', we should not know what was meant, or what sort of scientific test could be applied to such a proposition as 'Everything changes'. Science measures changes of particular sorts; and science might test the statement that a particular factor remains constant during a particular reaction. But 'This thing changes'—where would you begin in testing that? What sort of investigation would it be? Or if you say 'Nothing is permanent'—what sort of consequences follow? (I suppose you would still build buildings and select your materials as before. Just as you would still distinguish between a curable injury and a permanent injury.)

The point is that there is no sense in talking about 'bare' change or bare permanence, or in talking about 'change'— in some absolute sense—as something that 'goes on'. You can distinguish between the changing features and the permanent features in some situation. And you can talk about the changes which sulphur may undergo (though it is still sulphur). But if you say the permanent features there were 'really' changing, this is a misunderstanding, because you are now employing different criteria, and you seem to be suggesting that those features were not permanent after all—as though your former statement were false. You can distinguish between a crystalline state of sulphur and the process of melting sulphur. And if you say that the crystalline state is 'really a complex of processes', you have not removed the distinction nor made it clearer. You are concerned with a different sort of description—in terms of electrons or whatever it may be.

You may say that science is *interested* in changes, and that scientific laws are concerned with measurements and functional relations of changes. But this would not show that science ignores permanent features or permanent states, let alone showing that there are none. If it did, it could not describe the change that was being measured. And although science measures changes, it does not measure 'change'.

If you say nothing is absolutely permanent, well nothing is absolutely changing either. (Which is a statement about the use of these expressions, not a statement of what has been discovered.)

'Everything changes' may be the expression of a particular *mood*. At best it tells us something of how you *look* at things. It is not a scientific generalization.

'Science shows', it may be said, 'that everything has an origin and everything perishes'. This is rather like saying that science shows that everything has a cause. We may investigate to find out what the cause of an occurrence was, or what causes things of this sort. We do not investigate to see whether this occurrence had a cause or not, and we should not know what was meant by that. The causal generalizations of science state that such occurrences are caused in those ways. 'All occurrences are caused' is not a generalization of that kind, and it is not based on the results of any scientific inquiry. Similarly, we should not know what was meant by investigating to see whether something had an origin or not; though we may investigate to find what its origin was. No doubt we have good reason to *look* for the origins of things, because when we do we so often find them. But this sort of 'good reason' is not a scientific justification of the conclusion that everything *has* an origin. If you say—perhaps of atoms or of stellar nebulae—that 'Each *must* have had an origin', that is more like a slogan; it is not an empirical statement.

Suppose one said that science can calculate the age of everything and predict how long it will last. I do not know whether scientists would say this. But it would be similar to saying that there are scientific laws for everything. That might be said to express 'a scientific view of reality', in the sense that science could make nothing of any statement that there were some things for which no laws held. For that could have no connexion with or bearing on scientific statements, or on the scientist's distinction between what is so and what is not. And it might be said that 'There is nothing which has not a discoverable origin and a discoverable end' belongs to such a 'view of reality' also, since science could make nothing of the contradictory. But such a 'scientific view of reality' is not a *theory*. And it is not a scientific view in the sense in which a theory of heat or light is. Nor does science give any reasons for it as it does for those theories. It is not a scientific description of anything and it is not a conclusion that is drawn about anything. And to say here that 'science shows us what reality is like' could only be misleading. This 'scientific view of reality' is not part of what science shows.

In any case, granting that all things have origins and perish, this does not suggest anything like a universal process of change. And it does not suggest that changes are any more 'fundamental' than permanence is. Engels said that 'dialectical philosophy', with the support of 'modern natural science', 'reveals the transitory character of everything and in everything; nothing can endure before it except the uninterrupted (?) process of becoming and passing away'.[1] But I do not know what this 'process' is and the fact that all things originate and perish does not show anything of the sort. Coming to be and passing away is not a process at all. A process, I suppose, is something that may be des-

[1] *Ludwig Feuerbach*, translated in *Karl Marx, Selected Works*, London, 1942, vol. i, p. 422.

cribed, as a process of gestation might, or a process of decay, or a process of heating or cooling, or any chemical reaction. But what can you say of the process of becoming and passing away, which is supposed to be always going on? It is sometimes said that 'succession' or 'passage' is a fundamental feature of reality. I suppose the analogy is with the succession of seasons, or with the succession of phases in the growth of an organism, or with the succession of generations in a family. Here we have the succession of events in a process, or members of a series; we may call the succession of the seasons a cyclic process, and the succession of generations forms the history of the family or the 'life' of the family. But in all these cases the character of what appears is at least as important as its transitoriness; otherwise there would be no connexion between one event and what succeeds it, and we could not talk of a process at all. In fact, we always have in mind some process or other *before* we talk of succession. Succession itself is not a character of anything, and it means nothing to say that succession is a character of reality. Nor does the transitoriness of things show that reality is a process, or that it is any sort of change, or that it is *undergoing* any sort of change.

If you say 'The succession of events forms the history of the world', you are still employing the confusion and not removing it. 'The succession of events' means nothing by itself. It may look as though 'the history of the world' adds something; though that is partly because of an ambiguity, and it would be less plausible to speak of 'the history of reality'. When we speak generally of 'the history of England', for example, we do understand more or less vaguely what sort of events and changes are referred to, and we know certain general connexions between them. But we know nothing like this when we hear of 'the history of reality'. And the history of coming to be and passing away is nothing at all.

Cornforth seems to think that particular happenings and the particular changes we study are aspects of some universal change. This view may rest partly on the fact that in

physics the results that are reached are explained by reference to more general laws; so that the special laws may
appear to be instances or aspects of the more general laws.
But although such explanations may show you how certain
changes are interrelated as instances of a general type of
change—that they exhibit common features and so are comparable—this does not show that they are phases of an all
embracing change or process, or even that they are all interdependent. If the laws of mechanics can be applied to all
motions, that does not say that all motions are aspects of the
universal motion—as though that meant anything. Whatever might be meant by saying that the laws of mechanics
described the general features of the world, no 'universal
movement' could possibly be described in terms of them.
The proposition that all bodies move does not imply that
there is one movement in which they all participate. Nor,
incidentally, does it deny that bodies are ever at rest.

There is nothing, then, except confusion in the view that
change or process is in any way 'basic'. It is nothing that
science gives us any reason to believe. And it is no reason
for saying that science shows us the nature of the world
or the nature of reality.

You may say that science describes reality in the sense
that it shows you what really happens, as opposed to what
you might have imagined, in some particular case. If
someone thinks that he can maintain vigorous health for
several years without proteins, physiology may show him
(what he might find out the hard way) that his view is in
conflict with reality. So physiology tells you something
about reality. But it does not tell you what 'being real' is; or
tell you the nature of reality in that sense. And it is hard to
see that it has told you something about the nature of the
world.

But I think Cornforth would say it has. He seems to hold
that the particular results in physiology or elsewhere reveal
something 'further' about the nature of reality, because they
show you 'what is involved' in any more general reference
to 'reality as a whole'. If you could know what reality is

like, you would know all that science discovers. And science shows you gradually and progressively what reality is like. Only, of course, the new discoveries do not simply add to what you knew. They change your conception of reality. Perhaps this goes with his idea of a developing reality, or of 'changes in the whole character' of 'nature' (p. 217). In any case it implies that scientists do not mean the same by 'reality' or by 'existence' now as they did in earlier periods.

Now if there should be a fundamental change in methods of investigation—if scientists no longer looked for causes, for instance—then perhaps you could say that the conception of reality had changed. So would the idea of the solution of problems. But this different conception of reality would not be something that was revealed by the discoveries of science. If the meaning of 'reality' and of 'existence' changed with each discovery, how could you say that the discovery tells you something further about it? If 'discovery' and 'correction of errors' and 'testing' mean the same before the solution of a problem as after, then in one sense 'reality' does too, and so does 'existence'. So this sort of understanding is in some sense prior to scientific discoveries, and is not gained from them. And it is a confusion to say that progress in science is progress in the knowledge of the nature of reality. You can say it is progress in knowledge of what really is the case. But that is not knowledge of the nature of reality or the nature of the world.

The idea of learning more *about* reality is confused in any case just as the idea of a 'representation of reality' or a 'picture of the world' is, and as the idea of a more or less exact correspondence between this picture and reality also is. Cornforth thinks that science gives us such a picture, and that its correspondence with reality is becoming 'ever more accurate'. But if there were a different form of investigation—one not devoted to measurement of forces and to establishing functional dependence, for instance—what would be meant by saying that it did not correspond with or accord with reality? You might not be able to use it for predictions, as we use science. And 'explanation' would be something different, too. But if you did not try to use it for predictions in this way (because that was not what you were concerned about) with what reality would it be in discord? and what sort of discord would it be?

You might say it would 'conflict' with 'social practice', if social practice is devotion to the advancement of engineering and of industry. But can you say that social practice *is* the reality which science reveals or 'reflects'? especially if you want to say that social practice also reflects reality?

Cornforth's account of all this is confusing because he thinks that 'abstraction' is a kind of falsification and that you have to get rid of it if you want to see what is true. This confuses his account of the relation of science to social practice (i.e. to industry), and his account of the relation of both to 'the world'. He thinks that the 'pure empiricists' gave a false account of knowledge and of science because they regarded them 'in abstraction from all other human activities'. As opposed to this Cornforth is able to say that because problems of industry or social practice called the attention of scientists to problems in science, therefore 'basically' problems of science *are* problems of social practice (pp. 230, 231). ('Basically', like 'in the last analysis', is one of the expressions Marxists use to blur issues.) And this devotion to viewing things concretely as 'aspects' of the one process allows Cornforth to talk freely about what science 'reflects'. The aspect always reflects the whole; or if there are differences, they are again only different aspects of the whole. So science reflects what gave rise to it (it seems to reflect everything that is going on around it) and it also reflects all its possible applications. That all belongs to its 'objective import', and is part of what science really shows us.

But if that is how science 'shows us what the world is really like', then it does not arise from anything that science says. And we could not have learned from *science* that there was such a world, or that scientific activity was an 'aspect' of it.

One might even think that if abstraction is falsification,

then science never says anything that is true. In any case, it does not say any of the things about reality or about the world that Cornforth says it does. And Cornforth makes no headway in his criticisms of logical atomism by trying to show that science contradicts it. He only shows that he has misunderstood the sort of discussion that logical atomism was.

By 'logical atomism' Cornforth means the views expressed in Russell's *Our Knowledge of the External World* and in Wittgenstein's *Tractatus*. And he says 'the whole standpoint of logical atomism . . . is untenable, because it is impossible to find any atomic fact in the world, or to formulate any elementary proposition satisfying the postulates of the logical theory' (p. 140). But these two points are not the same. In the view of the *Tractatus* we can be sure there are atomic facts even if we are not sure of the forms of elementary propositions. And part of Cornforth's trouble is that he does not see the importance of this difference.

Cornforth assumes that an investigation must either be scientific or be pseudo-science. But discussions such as logical atomism was are neither. An inquiry into the nature of logic, or the nature of propositions, or of truth, or of knowledge, is an attempt to get clear about the usage of certain words, or to distinguish certain concepts. It is not an attempt to discover new facts which special methods now make accessible. The reasons for seeking a clarification of logic may be various. They may come from puzzles about mathematics, and about the relations between mathematics and logic. In any case, people have felt a deep unclarity about what logical conclusions are, what contradictions are, and what propositions are. And of course the attempt to get clear—to see what we are talking about here—has itself led to new puzzles and new difficulties. The search for clarification may lead people to look for definitions, as it has elsewhere in philosophy; as Socrates looked for a definition of knowledge, and as Russell tried to give a definition of a physical object in terms of perspectives and sense data. So perhaps logical atomism tried to give something like a definition of logic through analysis of logical forms and of symbols.

In much of philosophy such definitions seem to be misleading or not to serve for what is wanted, even though valuable work may have been done in trying to formulate them. (For instance, even if the attempts to define 'knowledge' only bring out that no definition really describes the whole usage, that there are no regular or fixed boundaries here, that is extremely important.) This seems to be so regarding 'proposition' and 'truth', and even regarding 'logical principles'. And the line that logical atomism took in trying to clarify these notions may have been largely wrong; though we should hardly see this now if the attempt had not been made. It may be that the reference to atomic facts and elementary propositions does not explain logic or make it clearer in the way it was meant to do. But to show this you have to do philosophy. You have to show *what* was wrong—what sort of mistake it was. And you do not do this by saying, as Cornforth does, that 'observation and experiment have never yet revealed any atomic fact'.

A 'theory of logic' would not have the same function, as a theory in physics. And if, in the course of it, it is said, for instance, that the world consists of atomic facts, this is clearly not a theory about the structure of things in the sense in which atomic theories in physics are. It is rather a theory of truth. And you might say it bears on physics only in questions of the relation of physics to logic. The reference to 'the world' in logical theory is part of the attempt to 'explain' logic in this way; to bring out the distinctions between logical laws and other propositions, to bring out what is meant by 'logical impossibility', what would be meant by calling logical principles 'laws of thought' and so on. It may be questioned whether the reference to 'the world' is really helpful here, and Wittgenstein no longer makes it. But where it appears in the earlier work of Wittgenstein and of Russell there is clearly nothing like a theory about what may be discovered through methods superior to those of science.

It is partly because he misunderstands this reference to 'the world' that Cornforth makes such a point of what he calls Wittgenstein's 'solipsism'. Wittgenstein has never held to solipsism, either in the *Tractatus* or at any other time. Cornforth may have been misled to some extent by a bad translation. In *Tractatus* 5. 62, Wittgenstein said, 'Was der Solipsismus nämlich *meint*, ist ganz richtig, nur lässt es sich nicht *sagen*, sondern es zeigt sich'. This is translated, 'In fact, what solipsism *means* is quite correct, only it cannot be *said*, but it shows itself'. And Cornforth frequently quotes only 'What solipsism means is quite correct' (without the italics) as though it were tantamount to saying that solipsism is quite correct. But the translation should rather be, 'What solipsism *wants* to say is quite correct'. For Wittgenstein was not saying that what solipsism *says* is correct in any way; in fact, he was denying that. But even with the bad translation Cornforth might have seen the point if he had looked more closely at the context in which Wittgenstein made the statement and at his reasons for making it. Wittgenstein was talking about 'the limits of our language'—about the limits of intelligibility, about the distinction between what makes sense and what does not. These limits are given in logic; and in the same way, the 'limits of the world', or limits of what can be, are given in logic. Only these limits cannot be *described*—just for the reason that they *are* limits of language or limits of intelligibility. They can only be seen or understood, in the way logic can. The discussion is connected with Wittgenstein's whole account of logical symbolism, with his view that logical constants do not 'represent' anything, and with what he says about internal relations and about how we know the structure of facts or the structure of the world. What logic shows about the world—the nature of reality in this sense, what it is to be a fact—is not something that can be said; any more than you can describe what a logical connexion is. Only if you say it has to be *seen*—then the limit is the limit of what can be seen, or rather the limit of *seeing*. The limit of understanding; and this is not something that can be found out by experience. Nor, of course, can it be compared with anything. 'That the world is my world', said Wittgenstein, 'shows itself in the fact that the limits of *that* language (the language which only I understand)[1] mean the limits of *my* world'. Of course Wittgenstein is not saying that all language, or everything about language, is something which only I understand, especially if you take 'I' to mean L. Wittgenstein or any other particular man. And what he says here does not run counter to what he says in other passages about colloquial language, for instance. What is important is logical symbolism. And his point is that the 'I' does not really stand for anything.

'The philosophical I', he said, 'is not the man, not the human body, or the human mind of which psychology treats, but the metaphysical subject, the limit—not a part of the world' (5. 641). And it is in this sense of the *limit* that he also says, 'I am my world'. (Cornforth misses the importance of the reference to 'the limit' here, and also in his quotation of Wittgenstein's statement that 'The world of the happy is another than the world of the unhappy'. Here again the point is not that the unhappy man knows or observes anything different from what happy people do.)

This is not a form of relativism or of 'subjectivism'; and it is not solipsism. In discussing the analogy with the visual field—and with 'the limits of seeing' in that sense—Wittgenstein says that you cannot infer from anything in the visual field that it is seen by an eye; and this is connected with the fact that nothing in our experience is *a priori* and that everything we see could also be otherwise. And in the same way, you cannot infer from anything you experience that it is experienced by a particular person, or even that it is experienced by a human being or any sort of organism or any sort of mind. That is why he says that if you try to work out solipsism it will coincide with pure realism.

It is nowhere implied in the *Tractatus* that in order to say *what* a proposition means I have to say what happens to me.

[1] This translation is wrong. Hintikka was right about this (*Mind* 1958, p. 88). Or see the Pears and McGuinness Translation, *Tractatus* 5.62.

And although Wittgenstein spoke of 'my world' in the connexions mentioned, he did not speak in any similar way of 'my experience'. Cornforth tries to show that Wittgenstein's views were solipsistic by bringing in 'the principle of verification'—the view that the meaning of a proposition is the method of its verification. Verification in this sense is not mentioned in the *Tractatus*. There are suggestions of it, which Cornforth points out, in such statements as, 'To understand a proposition means to know what is the case if it is true'. But in the first place, this does not bear on what Wittgenstein does say in reference to solipsism. And in the second place, there is nothing in such statements, or in what is said about atomic facts, to suggest that in order to say what is the case if it is true I must refer to *my sensations*, or even to 'my experience'. Yet Cornforth says that 'by means of the principle of verification, Wittgenstein has rigidly insisted that every "analysis" shall be in terms of the constituents of sense experience. . . . Every proposition, whether it is a simple statement of fact or a proposition of science, means only something about experience' (p. 158); and, 'It is clear already that when Wittgenstein said: "In order to discover whether the picture is true or false, *we* must compare it with *reality*", what he means would be better expressed: "In order to discover whether the picture is true or false, *I* must compare it with *my experience*" ' (p. 150). I do not know whether Cornforth has read what Wittgenstein did say in the *Tractatus* about propositions of science, or what he would make, e.g. of the statement there that 'Through the whole apparatus of logic the physical laws still speak of the objects of the world' (6. 3431). In any case nothing is said there, and I do not think anything was ever said by Wittgenstein, to bear out the conclusions which Cornforth tries to draw from 'the principle of verification'. He argues—as Wittgenstein would have agreed—that in science verification is often carried out by several people working together, and that it cannot be 'the work of one person in a solipsistic world of his own'; and Wittgenstein never said nor implied that it could.

Cornforth misrepresents Wittgenstein's views more commonly perhaps, than he does those of the other philosophers he discusses. But for the most part the misrepresentations are obvious enough to need no comment. The main point is that he does not see what Wittgenstein was saying. And this may be partly because he thinks that all philosophy is devoted to affirming 'the independent existence of the objective material world of which science treats', or else to denying it.

Cornforth's most important issue with Carnap is regarding the nature of logical principles, and in particular regarding what Carnap said about 'the principle of tolerance' and the question of 'the true logic'. Cornforth insists against him that the principles of logic 'conform to the world of being, and to the logic of that world'. 'Propositions represent things. . . . Propositions communicate information. And the principles of logic do accordingly possess an objective validity, or, if you like "constitute a faithful rendering of the true logic", in the sense that they show, given certain information, what further is involved or follows from it. The validity of logical principles results from this, that the information expressed in the conclusion is involved in or contained in the information expressed in the premisses.' They therefore, 'represent something more than just syntactical "rules of formation and transformation"' (pp. 199, 200).

Here there is some play with the ambiguity of 'involved in'. But the point seems to be that because in arguments— the arguments in which we 'employ' logic—we are talking about things and events, therefore logical principles or logical relations must correspond to some relations among things and events.

But an argument is not a description of anything even though descriptions may occur in it. And although calculations may show you how things will be, and your predictions may be confirmed, this does not corroborate your calculation.

You can say, I think, that our logic 'has something to do with' the sorts of things we talk about, just as the character of arithmetic has, and as our language altogether has. If things were entirely different and behaved entirely differently—if one could never speak of identity in the way we do, for instance, or make the sorts of distinctions among things that we do—people might never have come to reason as we do. But that is not to say that our principles of reasoning describe the sorts of things we talk about; though they may play a part in determining what we should call a description and what not. But if the description were 'incorrect' from this point of view, it would not be because it had said anything about reality which did not correspond to it.

If you say that logical principles are rules of syntax, that seems in a way superficial, especially if you do not discuss the sort of syntax that is in question. And to talk about *choosing* our language or *choosing* our logic is silly, if only because *choosing* belongs to the 'language'—the way of living and speaking—which *has* the logic we know. Which is not to say that a society might not live and speak differently—or do something analogous to speaking, if you wish to say that without our logic you would not call it speaking. (This is one of the points which Wittgenstein has made, I think.) And for similar reasons I think it is misleading to talk about a 'principle of tolerance' in logic. It is true that no one deductive system is *the* true representation of our actual use of logical principles; and that this will never be so. But the question of 'the truth of logic' is not always a question of the truth of a deductive system, and 'the truth of logical principles' does not always mean truth within a deductive system. And the reference to 'alternative logics'—to 'two valued' and 'many valued logics' and so on—confuses the issues here. The alternative logics may be important in showing that you can calculate according to various rules and you would still call it calculation. Also perhaps that what you would call contradiction in one system you would not call contradiction in another. They may have made clearer what 'being logical' or 'being a calculus' consists in, and shown that certain things are not essential. But the alternative logics are all supposed, I think, to be deductive systems, and in that sense they are all supposed to be logical. They do not question the distinction between logical and illogical procedure. And as far as I can see they do not touch the question of 'whether there could be an illogical world' or the question of the truth of logic in the sense of the 'truth' of standards distinguishing between logical and illogical. I do not think, either, that you can settle many important philosophical questions about the nature of logical necessity or the nature of proof by reference to them.

These questions are too difficult for treatment here. But if Carnap's discussion of them was unsatisfactory, it was not because he said that logical principles are rules of syntax instead of saying that they tell you something about the material world.

These are samples of what I think are central among the problems Cornforth treats.

His account of the 'social function' of philosophy is not worked out, and it is infected with the confusions I have mentioned. The task of philosophy, he says, is to show that science solves the problems of philosophy. In doing this philosophy shows that science can change the world. And so it shows mankind how science can make it master of its destiny.

Cornforth thinks that if you admit that science provides knowledge of the world, you must admit that science can change the world; though really it does not follow. And if science could change the world, it would not mean that 'mankind' was master of its destiny. His position is too vaguely stated for full criticism. The following are points among many which Cornforth might have considered.

(*a*) It is not true that when you discover something in science you thereby gain power to change it. The changes you make in things may depend on scientific discoveries. But unless you discovered something you *cannot* change, you could not predict, and there could be no engineering.[1]

(*b*) Your power to change the world may be limited by

[1] Cf. J. A. Passmore, 'Prediction and Scientific Law', *The Australasian Journal of Psychology and Philosophy*, September 1946.

the fact that someone else, who also has knowledge, is trying to change it in a different way.

(*c*) There is nothing about human societies which makes it reasonable to speak of the application of engineering to them. Even the most important 'problems of production' are not problems of engineering.

(*d*) Though scientists may 'lay the foundations' for the work of those who will come after them, they do not control it.

(*e*) There are various sorts of 'social practice' and there is no reason why 'solving problems of social practice' should lead to the liberation of humanity from poverty and oppression. Nor would the application of science to social practice make this likely. Science may be used in preserving privilege and intensifying oppression.

4

'Social Engineering'

'The only course open to the social sciences', says Dr. Popper, 'is . . . to tackle the practical problems of our time with the help of the theoretical methods which are fundamentally the same in *all* sciences. . . . A social technology is needed which can be tested by social engineering'[1].

On this view, then, the social sciences are concerned with 'practical problems'. And although these differ from theoretical problems, the assumption is that the same methods may be used for solving them.

But there are important differences. 'The social engineer believes that man is the master of his own destiny, and that in accordance with our aims we can influence or change the history of man just as we have changed the face of the earth' (vol. i, p. 17). But the history of man is fundamentally different from the face of the earth, and so is the science of it. 'The beginning of social science . . . is marked by the distinction between two different elements in man's environment—his natural environment and his social environment.' For there can be no social science until there is a clear grasp of the fundamental distinction between '(*a*) *natural laws*, or laws of nature, or positive laws, such as the law of the apparent motion of the sun, or the law of gravity; and (*b*) *normative laws*, or standards, or norms, i.e. rules that forbid or demand certain modes of conduct, or certain procedures; examples are the laws of the Athenian Con-

[1] *The Open Society and its Enemies*, London, 1945, vol. ii, p. 210.

stitution, or the rules pertaining to the election of Members of Parliament, or the Ten Commandments' (vol. i, p. 49). These normative laws are 'decisions' and are man-made. Natural laws are independent of us. This is part of what Popper calls the 'dualism of facts and decisions'.

Granting that these are different senses of 'law', it might still seem misleading to say that natural science studies natural laws, while social science studies normative laws. No doubt the study of society takes account of norms and standards, and of how they operate—how they arise, and how they influence social developments. But then it is studying them as natural, and if it succeeds in giving any general account of their operation it is formulating natural laws.

But Popper is not thinking of the *study* of society when he speaks of social science. He is thinking of the 'scientific' *changing* of it—of the solution of 'practical problems'. That is why he thinks that if the social sciences were scientific they would be forms of social engineering.

Not all his statements about this are consistent. Towards the beginning of his book he suggests that a social engineer merely asks whether a particular institution is 'well designed and organized to serve' any aims which have been proposed. 'In his function as a citizen, who has certain ends in which he believes, he may demand that these ends, and the appropriate measures, should be adopted. But as a technologist, he would carefully distinguish between the question of the ends and their choice and questions concerning the facts, i.e. the social effects of any measure which might be taken' (vol. i, p. 19). But he generally speaks as though it were the business of social engineers to 'reform' social institutions. It is to this end that they perform 'social experiments'. Their problems are problems of how to 'improve civilization'. 'The "world"', he says (vol. ii, p. 337), 'is not rational, but it is the task of science to rationalize it. "Society" is not rational, but it is the task of the social engineer to rationalize it'. By 'rationalizing the world' I suppose he means *understanding* the world, or giving an account of it. But he does not mean that the social engineer should try only to understand society. His point is that rationalizing society is altering or improving it. That is clear from the whole of chapter 24.

So when Popper speaks of making the social sciences scientific he generally means making social *policy* scientific.[1] He is holding that there is an analogy between 'problems of social policy' and problems of science; and that they may be solved by the same methods. The science and discussion of social affairs will be a discussion of norms and of decisions; it will be a matter of justifying decisions or criticizing them. It will include the critical discussion of institutions. But progress in such discussion will be progress in working out a policy for institutions, not a theory of them.

For I take it that the dualism of facts and decisions means, for Popper, that decisions must be studied differently. That is part of what is meant by saying that they cannot be reduced to facts. I may decide that it is wrong to steal. Then my deciding is a fact, but 'It's wrong to steal' is not a fact. It is not something to be *believed*. It is something that has to be *decided*—for or against. And the utterance of it is not the expression of a belief but of a decision. If I try to influence another in respect of such utterances, I try to influence his will or his decisions, not his beliefs. I could not *disprove* his decision that it is wrong to steal, or show that it was mistaken; at least not in the way in which I might show that his beliefs about matters of fact were mistaken. I may point out to him certain consequences. But 'the decision depends on him'.

Popper's discussion of all this is confusing, and I do not know how near my paraphrase comes. But he wants to hold, I think, that *because* 'decisions or norms' cannot be reduced to facts, social science is a practical inquiry. To improve its method we must bring scientific method to decisions; at least when they are decisions of public policy.

[1] On the common confusion between social theory and policy see J. Anderson, 'Utilitarianism', *The Australasian Journal of Psychology and Philosophy*, September 1932, p. 167. I am indebted to other articles by Professor Anderson and others of his school in the same journal.

The dualism of facts and decisions implies also that 'existing normative laws (or social institutions)' (vol. i, p. 52) depend on 'us'. It is 'we' who create or adopt them, and their existence cannot result from anything but our decision to create or adopt them. The dualism—the distinction between a mechanistic and a voluntaristic realm—is needed for the view that man is the master of his destiny and that society can be shaped and controlled by social engineering. But there are complications. We must apply engineering to social institutions. Yet it is hard to think of applying it to decisions. And we find that institutions are really a combination of normative laws and natural laws. 'There are important natural laws in social life also. For these the term "sociological laws" seems appropriate. . . . In institutions normative laws and sociological laws are closely interwoven,[1] and it is therefore impossible to understand the functioning of institutions without being able to distinguish between these two' (vol. i, pp. 56, 57).

There is such a dualism in institutions that Popper says different things about them. At first he uses 'normative laws' and 'social institutions' as equivalent. He says that institutions are norms or standards which we adopt and for which we are morally responsible. But he sometimes speaks of them as machines that need intelligent supervision, or as fortresses which must be manned. His main view seems to be that they are *instruments* which 'we' may use for good or evil.

When he is speaking of them as something for which we are morally responsible, he equates institutions with conventions and so with normative laws and so with norms. 'Norms and normative laws can be made and changed by man, more especially by a decision or convention to observe them or to alter them, and it is therefore man who is morally responsible for them; not perhaps for the norms which he finds to exist in society when he first begins to reflect on them, but for the norms which he is prepared to tolerate

[1] The phrase 'closely interwoven' covers a good many difficulties, and hardly makes the 'dualism' clearer.

once he has found out that he can do something to alter them. Norms are man-made in the sense that we must blame nobody but ourselves for them' (vol. i, p. 51).

Here, and throughout the book, Popper is ruthless with 'man' and 'we'. 'Social institutions have been made by man' may mean only that they have arisen in the histories of human societies, or that their development is a development of human and social activities. It may mean also that they are not 'fixed' as say, human anatomy is. But this would not mean that they have arisen because anyone decided to create them, or that they persist—when they do—because anyone has decided to maintain them. Nor does it give ground for saying that 'the responsibility for them is entirely ours'. To say that 'man' is morally responsible for anything is meaningless; just as it is to say that 'man' has made a decision. But this sort of confusion helps Popper to combine an historical with a voluntarist view of society (and to hold that man makes his history, which is a history *of* his making although his making is not made).

But the passage has a further interest. It is not at first sight clear why dualism should be as important for social science as Popper says it is. There can be no social engineering unless normative laws or social institutions can be made and changed by man. But machines can also be made by man, and we have changed the face of the earth; and these are not norms. So why cannot social science hold that normative laws can be made and changed without holding to a dualism of norms and facts? Popper gives one answer when he explains that to say we make norms means that we are morally responsible for them—'that we alone carry the responsibility for adopting them'. The earth is not responsible for the changes wrought in its face, but we are responsible for the changes in the society in which we live. Theories of social engineering have been criticized on the ground that the 'engineer' must be subject to the influences he is trying to control. But this does not alter his responsibility. He is responsible even for the ways in which those influences—existing norms—affect him. And if he tries to alter them, the way in which he does this depends entirely upon him; it is his responsibility. Social engineering is possible if you recognize this character of normative laws or institutions—this sort of 'dependence on us' which they have; and it would not be possible otherwise.

This account of what is meant by 'making' normative laws or institutions leaves the analogy with mechanical engineering rather thin. But I do not think Popper could hold to social engineering without it.

Still, when he is emphasizing the instrumental character of institutions and comparing them with machines, this feature of their dependence is left more in the background. 'Institutions are always made by establishing the observance of certain norms, designed with a certain aim in mind. . . . Like machines, they need intelligent supervision by someone who understands their way of functioning and, most of all, their purpose, since we cannot build them so that they work entirely automatically' (vol. i, p. 56). 'The engineer or the technologist approaches institutions rationally as means that serve certain ends . . . as a technologist he judges them wholly according to their appropriateness, efficiency, simplicity, etc.' (vol. i, p. 19). Here he mentions insurance and a police force as examples. But he would clearly regard political institutions, penal systems, educational institutions, trade unions, banking institutions, scientific institutions and so on, in the same way.

I see no reason to believe that all institutions have been 'designed with a certain aim in mind'. Why should one say this of penal systems, for instance, or of many legal institutions? One might argue that they have not been designed at all, any more than language has. But anyway, as they exist now, there is apparently no *one* aim for which people support them. That is why you cannot give *the* reason why we have a public penal system, for instance. Some may advocate punishing criminals because they deserve it, others say it is needed as a deterrent, or they may give other utilitarian or sociological justifications. This is true of statesmen as well as laymen. But the penal system is there and it is carried on in that way, and it is generally supported. Similar remarks might be made of other institutions. Even when they have grown from beginnings which were designed with a certain aim in mind, the design cannot generally have included much of their present development; and it does not account for much. They have been supported and taken over and developed by influences and new developments that had no part in their beginning. And of course for the most part we simply support such institutions because they *are* there, and not because we have any aim or reason in doing so; so with property rights, contract, taxation, and so on.

So why talk of 'the purpose' of social institutions? What is the purpose of educational institutions, for instance? or, if you like, what is 'the aim of education'? Those who work in education may believe they are training people for 'life', or making them better able to fend for themselves, or that they are trying to develop personalities, or that they are training them for citizenship or merely that they are trying to give them good schooling. Such ideas may conflict, and there may be conflicts within educational institutions. But they will go on just the same.

Possibly you can talk of the purpose of a standing army; and perhaps of a police force. (Though in neither case would this be quite simple.) I do not think you can talk of the purpose of banks, though of course you would go to them for certain things and not for others. Trade unions may become 'organs of struggle' or they may become organizations for negotiating with employers and administering relief. I should not know what was meant by their 'purpose'. And what is the purpose of the theatre?

It might be answered that the purpose of the theatre is to produce drama; as it might be said that the purpose of universities is to carry on academic work. These answers would be disputed. And in a sense they are denying that there is any purpose. But such answers suggest standards of good work or of serious work in these fields. And it might be argued that unless there is concern for these standards the institutions may die out or lose any distinctive character that they have. I do not know whether this is true. But in any case it is a different proposition from Popper's view that institutions 'need intelligent supervision'.

There are conflicting tendencies in the working of any institution. But there are common ways of working there too. Otherwise the institution could not go on. And this makes it possible for those engaged in them to discuss and formulate policies for institutions (even though some opposition may remain to any declared policy). But that does not mean that the institutions are 'means' which 'serve the ends' of those engaged in them. Banking institutions are not merely instruments of those engaged in their operation. These people may make decisions in the course of their work and may contribute to the framing of policies. But these are *banking* policies, policies *of* the institutions. They are not statements of ends that banking institutions are to be used for. And similarly elsewhere.

This is obscured by Popper's statement that 'the functioning of even the best institutions will always depend, to a considerable degree, on its personnel. Institutions are like fortresses. They must be well designed *and* manned. . . . They cannot improve themselves. The problem of improving them is always a problem of persons rather than of institutions' (vol. i, pp. 110, 111). This idea of 'manning' institutions, as men man fortresses or man machines, is misleading. (An army may man a fortress but do the soldiers 'man' the army?) And it leads here to a false distinction between personnel problems and problems of institutions. We are told that an individual might improve an institution by working hard and setting a good example. I doubt if Popper means just this. Yet apart from this the improvement of institutions is not a matter of individual decisions and individual conscience.

And in suggesting that the institution is controlled by those who man it, and that their plans and norms and decisions are not controlled by *it*—almost as if the working of the institution itself had nothing to do with decisions and projects, as if they were no more part of that working than they are of the working of a machine—Popper is also implying that just as the effect of the machine, what it accomplishes at any time, depends on the use we put it to, so it is too with institutions. Yet the contrast between the work a machine does and the influence of a social institution is really greater than the analogy. And for reasons similar to those which interfere with the notion that institutions are manned. You can use a bulldozer for various things, or you can leave it in the garage. But with most institutions it is not like that. The sort of influence they have is largely independent of any plans we may have for them, or any use we may wish to put them to. And this is just because they *are* institutions and are not machines. They are features or forms of social existence, not instruments of it. New institutions may develop—and existing institutions may change— *with* the development of machines. So with the development of printing, telephones, means of transport, wireless, motion pictures and many others. But even so there is no control of the institutions parallel to the control of the machines.

It is sometimes said of radio that 'radio is all right; it all depends on what you do with it'. But it is not simply that 'what you do with it' is limited by the special conditions of broadcasting. Radio is *there*, and it affects the lives of people in ways that do not depend upon policies of the board of governors. The fact that broadcast material, of whatever sort, comes into the homes in this way; the fact that people want to have it always on, as a background to what they are doing; that music is 'on tap', to be turned on and off; that broadcasting makes public utterances something different from what they were—these and countless other features of it—including the fact that people cannot do without it— influence public and private living and the development of norms and 'needs' and attitudes. The fact that people have become dependent upon radio and feel lost without it means that its influence is something more than that of an instrument which 'we' may use to exert our good or evil influence.

When Popper says that institutions 'need intelligent supervision', he thinks chiefly of supervision by those with political power. (That is who 'we' are, or should be.) And in much of his discussion it is mainly political institutions he has in mind.

But political control never wholly determines the development of other institutions; though of course it influences them. And political institutions are not just instruments themselves. They influence the character of political activities and decisions. This holds, first, of the institution of state power altogether ('all power corrupts'). There is, I think, no 'purpose' of the state, no 'true end of government'. But state power not only makes it possible to enforce particular policies or insure their domination in the society. It also influences the type of policies that are enforced. It affects the life of the society altogether, though with some forms of constitution more, with others less; and affects the sort of policies that arise there. But especially it affects the policies of those who are possessed of it. However strong other influences, say economic tendencies, may be, there is no doubt that state power has a rôle of its own, has tendencies of its own which 'catch up' those who arrive at it. Of course these tendencies grow and change with other social developments. But the state is no more just a means or instrument than religion is.

And special political institutions (representative institutions, institutions connected with hereditary monarchy, hierarchical organization and so on) are not just instruments either. They affect the character of political activities and programmes. The publicity of legislation influences the character of legislation and the sort of control that governments seek to exercise. A custom of parliamentary manoeuvring and intrigue may influence the way government is carried on and help to form standards of what is permissible among popular activities.

Popper's 'technological' view of such institutions is in line with the Marxist view of politics which he criticizes. Of course he cannot hold that institutions are through and through manipulated. That is why he says that there are 'important sociological laws connected with the functioning of social institutions'. But he holds that 'these laws play a rôle in our social life corresponding to the rôle played in mechanical engineering by, say, the principle of the lever' (vol. i, p. 56). And he will not admit that the formation of policies and decisions is *part* of the working of institutions. Decisions always depend on 'us' who 'supervise' them.

He seems to think that otherwise we should have to say that 'there is no escape' from the tendencies of existing institutions, and that institutions can never be 'reformed'. But that would be so only if we overlooked the ways in which institutions interact, and the ways in which the working of any institution may be interfered with and altered by developments from without.

To say that men's activities are largely shaped by the institutions they work in, is not to say that any man's activities are wholly shaped by the working of any *one* institution (a branch of scientific research, or trade union work, say), or that influences from elsewhere may not operate in him as powerfully. It is partly because they do, that we find interactions and rival tendencies within any institution. These differences help to make the history of any institution contingent[1] (as other social developments do also). But it is no help in understanding them if you say that men's consciences speak differently, and leave it at that.

In any case, you do not control the development of an institution by 'improving' or reforming it. Engineers may make a series of improvements in the design of a machine; and then the way the machine develops depends on the engineers. This is partly because the machine will not show important developments without them. But it would be a more relevant analogy here to say that the way *engineering* develops depends on the engineers.

---

[1] This 'contingency' does not imply indeterminism. The point is that the outcome depends on what happens, and there is not one outcome which is 'necessary'. See P. H. Partridge, 'Contingency', *The Australasian Journal of Psychology and Philosophy*, April 1938.

Now Popper seems to think it does. His reason for think-ing that we can control the development of institutions and progressively improve them seems to lie mainly in his view that in science we have an example of an institution which controls its own development and insures its own progress. So he thinks that if you introduce the methods of science into other institutions, and especially into politics, they will be sure of progress too. We may control our destiny if only we are scientific.

If in engineering, or in any science, the methods employed do not lead to a solution of the problems, the methods themselves are criticized. And they are criticized by the methods common to scientific inquiry. This criticism is possible—as in fact the maintenance of scientific method is possible—because of the social character of science; because of the fact that scientific work is always connected with scientific institutions—laboratories, periodicals, con-gresses—in which many different workers are engaged. It is in these institutions that the standards of objective criticism grow up and live (vol. ii, pp. 205 ff.).

No doubt this publicity and criticism of methods does help to maintain certain standards of scientific investigation. But these standards may be maintained while others change. Attention may come to be directed to certain fea-tures of experimental work at the expense of others. And in particular, there may be a change in the sort of problems that are regarded as important. There is nothing in the social character of scientific institutions or in their devotion to experimental techniques to prevent this. Judged by cer-tain standards, science may degenerate, however great the 'objectivity' that is maintained in it. This seems to have happened as science has been dominated more and more by technology and by 'practical' requirements.[1] There has

---

[1] Anderson remarks that in recent times ' "scientific advance" has been largely bound up with the decline of inquiry, that modern science does not exemplify disinterested inquiry. Its spirit has been "practical", it has been concerned with "getting things done", with facilitating transformations and

been a change in the dominant interest and in the character
of the work in scientific institutions. And this sort of change
cannot be 'corrected' by applying 'scientific method'.

The neglect or disregard of the degeneration of science is
connected with the view that science is all a matter of 'the
method'. This is a view that Popper explicitly shares. It is
fundamental to his view that the development of science is
self-controlling. But it is a naïve sort of view. It is like
confusing morality with precision.

You do not control the development of technology by
keeping it technological either. The same can be said of
anything that Popper calls 'social engineering'. And in this
case there is not really even the sort of control which the
sciences do have. Popper thinks you have begun to introduce engineering into social institutions when you have
public control through free criticism, as in science; and
when the institutions employ 'the methods of trial and
error, of inventing hypotheses which can be practically
tested, and of submitting them to practical tests' (vol. ii, p.
210). If politicians began 'to look out for their own
mistakes instead of trying to explain them away . . . this
would mean the introduction of scientific method into
politics, since the whole secret of scientific method is a
readiness to learn from mistakes' (vol. i, p. 144). But free
criticism has not the function in social affairs that it has in
science. And experimenting and learning by mistakes are
not the same here either. These points are both connected
with the fact that controversies in social affairs are not about
the solution of problems, as they are in science. If we speak
of 'social problems', that is something different.

Public criticism need not be anything like science. Consider literary criticism, for instance; or ethical criticism.
Popper might say literary criticism is not criticism of public
policy. But neither is scientific criticism. And he has not

---

translations, not just with finding out what is the case and with the "criticism
of categories" that that involves.' *Australasian Journal of Psychology and
Philosophy*, December 1945.

shown any clearer analogy in the one case than in the other. In fact, policies are criticized on *various* grounds. And the criticism may well be moral.

'Criticism', then, is not one thing. Men criticize in different ways and by different standards. And policies are defended in different ways and with different sorts of reasons. Scientific institutions function as they do because scientists agree as to the sort of evidence that justifies a conclusion or upsets it. But the sort of thing that justifies a social policy to some people may be no justification at all to others. (Compare the pacifist reaction to the justification of going to war; or the other way about. Or consider discussions as to whether strike-breaking is justified.)

Criticism may lead men to alter policies. And reasons may lead men to adopt them. But often they do not. When they do it is not like science. Arguing for a policy is not like establishing a theory, and raising objections to a policy is not like criticizing a theory. In any case, if 'public control through free criticism' means control by all citizens, this is unlike science because there are not common standards and methods of criticizing social policies.

Popper seems to think that 'potentially' there are. He thinks this follows from the social nature of argument and of reason. 'We owe our reason, like our language', he says, 'to intercourse with other men'; and so 'we must recognize everybody with whom we communicate as potentially a source of argument and of reasonable information'. This 'establishes what may be described as "the rational unity of mankind" ' (vol. ii, p. 213).

But we do not owe our reason, nor our language, to intercourse with *all* other men. We do not assume the same sort of argumentation or the same standards of criticism in all connexions. Nor do all men argue alike, especially about social matters. And there is nothing in the social character of argumentation to suggest that they ever will.

Men are led to policies, as they are to social movements or 'causes', by other factors than arguments. The influence is likely to be the other way. The movements in which they are associated do much to determine their standards and ways of arguing. Popper recognizes this when he speaks of the institutional or social character of scientific thinking. And it is not scientific reasoning that leads men first to take up science. Men enter different movements without reasons, and even without deciding to. And the different views they voice on social matters do not finally rest on reasons either.

So men may well hold to their views and proceed by their standards, no matter what arguments they meet. And if 'social problems' are conflicts of social policies and movements, there is no ground to think that arguments will 'solve' them. Discussion may be important. It may clarify issues—bring out 'what is involved'. This is sometimes needed before people can decide what attitude to take to some proposal. In general, discussion may make reactions less ambiguous (though it may work the other way). It may alter decisions, too. A man may wonder whether his decision was the right one (where to say he was 'mistaken' would mean that he would have chosen differently if he had seen more). And you can influence the decisions of others, in certain cases, if you make the issues clearer to them. But this may not lead to a decision in your favour. And it will not remove all conflicts.

Public criticism may further publicity in social affairs and help to bring out what the various aims and movements are. For this reason it is favoured by some movements and discouraged by others. But this publicity will not settle any problem, in the sense either of resolving the conflict or discovering what the outcome will be.

'The method of discussion' sometimes refers to the conference table, and negotiations. These discussions consist largely in sounding views or demands, and seeing what concessions may be made. This sometimes leads to 'an arrangement which all parties accept'; and then a 'solution' has been reached. But this 'general acceptability' is not like the objectivity of science. It depends on the way demands are pressed and what the parties are willing to concede in order to reach an understanding. You may say they wish to avoid conflict, and so their procedure is 'reasonable'. But this does not play the part of public control in scientific institutions.

Popper says the 'critical rationalism' he advocates 'suggests the idea that nobody should be his own judge, and it suggests the idea of impartiality'. And 'this is closely related to the idea of "scientific objectivity" ' (vol. ii, p. 225).

But granting that there are analogies between judicial procedures and scientific objectivity, what has this to do with political controversy? In the courts it is concerned with the effort to determine the facts of the case, and see how they stand in relation to the law. Even so it does not control or determine the *development* of law. One would not speak of scientific objectivity when a judge assesses the importance of claims and interests. In fact, on these questions judges *do* enter political controversy. And while they are not pressing personal considerations—social conflicts are not personal disputes anyway—they are voicing a particular school of thought or current of opinion on social matters. There is no 'impartiality that is closely related to scientific objectivity' on such issues. And we should not know what was meant by saying that there was.

This bears on the further point, that you cannot count on settling such differences by appealing to experience. Popper knows that what he calls 'social experiments' can never be used in social policy as physical experiments are used in engineering, if only because they are not framed so that they can be accurately repeated. But the main point is that in social matters the experiments do not decide the issue. If you speak of learning from experience here, it is a different sort of 'learning'. It means being made wiser, and you expect to see the result in conduct and in future policies. It is not like the case in which a scientist learns more about the behaviour of some material. This is the point of Popper's 'dualism of facts and decisions', or part of it. And in speaking of the 'analysis of the consequences of a moral theory' he says it 'has a certain analogy to scientific method. . . . But there is a fundamental difference. In the case of a scientific theory, our decision depends upon the results of the experiments. . . . But in the case of a moral theory we can only confront its consequences with our conscience. And while the verdict of experiments does not depend upon ourselves, the verdict of our conscience does' (vol. ii, p. 220). The same fundamental difference would hold for any adoption of a policy, I suppose. But scientific objectivity surely rests on the fact that in science the experiments *do* decide. And if there is nothing like that in social affairs, or in the settling of social problems, then what has scientific method to do with their solution?

For Popper, however, the real social problems are not conflicts; for these are not fundamental. The real problems are problems of improvement. The aim of social engineering is to 'improve matters', 'improve the lot of man' and 'improve civilization'.

'Improvement', like 'the common good', implies an all-embracing social aim or movement. It is a matter of furthering the cause of society as a whole. Popper speaks of the 'aim of civilization' (vol. i, p. 1). Social engineering is just the scientific way of furthering this aim. And 'piecemeal engineering' takes a no less 'monistic'view of society than 'total engineering' does. It plans to improve society as a whole—to make it a more 'rational' society—even though it will do this one step at a time. It is the cause of all mankind.

But we do not know what sort of enterprise this would be. As if there were some definite form of activity which was working for society; as if 'furthering society' meant anything. Yet if that means nothing, then neither does 'improving society'.

If there are conflicting ways of living, then no sort of work is working for society.

If there were not rival ways of living,[1] if there were not

---

[1] This conception of 'ways of living' I have taken mainly from Anderson. Wittgenstein uses the phrase in a somewhat different, but I think related, connexion.

conflicting movements, there would not be society as we know it. Any way of living is social. And accordingly it is involved in interaction and rivalry with others. This is characteristic of social existence, and we should not call anything social without it.

Humanitarianism is not a policy for society as a whole, in the sense of being a policy for all movements. It is a policy for protecting the weak; Popper calls it 'protectionism'. It pretends to universality by being a policy for all *men*, by being concerned about their 'lot'; and thus by disregarding different movements or ways of living.

With humanitarianism the dualism of decisions and facts appears in society too. And we find a distinction between those who decide and those who are protected (because they are too weak to decide).

This is not society controlling its own development. It is the domination of society by a particular group. (Whether you call it science is a matter of wisdom in advertising.) And in proportion as men do participate in running their own affairs, they will come in conflict with humanitarians and with the reasonableness of social engineers.

The idea of a 'social technology' rests on confusions about 'dependence'.

You cannot deduce principles and policies from the facts of science. And you cannot deduce the future from 'the nature of historical development'. But it does not follow that the future depends on what we decide. Nor does it follow that the principles we adopt depend only on us— unless that is just a tautology. (Popper repeats 'it is always *we* who decide', and he seems to think something important follows from this.) Generally we do not *adopt* principles at all. And the working of institutions does not depend upon what principles we decide to adopt. There is some voluntary activity in the functioning of institutions. So there is in language. But we do not make the language we speak. Nor does its persistence depend on our decisions. Neither do the activities for which policies are put forward—industry, education and the rest. Policies are put forward in the day's work.

And although you cannot deduce policies from facts, this does not point to a special realm in which special sorts of 'laws' hold. And there is no special science—a 'practical' science—of such laws.

5

Politics and Science

Puzzles about the nature of political power have made it hard to see what ruling is. And they have made it easier to think that political science might make ruling scientific.

There is a difference between political power and any other power in a society. For it is the power of a public authority. In that way it is unlike the power of wealth or of military organization, for instance.

When men recognize the authority of the state, they generally have no reason—except perhaps that everyone does and apparently always has. There may be reasons for recognizing this or that government. But then you take some authority of this kind for granted. And there are no comparable reasons for that. I think it would be absurd to ask for reasons which give the state its authority, just as it would be to ask this of any other authority.[1] (The authority of experts in scientific and other fields is obviously something different.) That it is exercised in some sense on behalf of the society, or that it is the power of the society, is the *sense* of the authority; not a reason for it.

The social contract theorists and utilitarians tried to rationalize some of this by arguing that there must be a state to preserve justice, or to direct affairs for the good of

[1] 'La philosophie est aussi incapable de démontrer le Gouvernement que de prouver Dieu. L'Autorité, comme la Divinité, n'est point matière de savoir; c'est, je le répète, matière de foi.' P.-J. Proudhon, *Les Confessions d'un Révolutionnaire*, Préface.

all (without quite explaining why states generally do neither). This is a kind of normative view of the state, and really tries to show how state power might be justified. But then it appears that anybody would be justified in using power to these ends. And the distinction between political power and private power is left obscure. The 'justification' of state power neither explains nor describes state authority.

Engels did more. But he still would have it that the state has a *function*, and even that it was *invented* in response to certain needs (*Origin of the Family*, end of Chapter IV). That reminds one of the contract theorists. But I think it is absurd. You cannot *invent* a public authority, which is really to be one.

If modern states are said to be necessary for the administration of 'essential services', we may ask how state administration differs from private administration of these services. And if state authority is needed for this work, the necessity of the work is not the source of state authority.

But if you leave explanations, and just ask 'What is political power?' that is puzzling enough. It may lead to questions like 'What are we obeying?', 'What are we subject to?', and to answers like 'We are obeying ourselves', or 'We are obeying the will of society as a whole'. Those are not good answers, but they recognize that the force is a public force in some peculiar way. The force or power of the government is in a way the force of the society one is living in. That is a vague idea, but it has some root in the way political power is exercised.

The power of the state is largely the power of other social forces there. It is because the military forces depend upon support, and because the owners of land and industry depend upon protection, that the state can control both. This sort of control grows as activities within the society become more specialized and more interdependent. For then whatever one does, one is less independent, and, it may seem, more dependent on state control.

So the force of government does reside considerably in 'divide et impera', and also in 'the needs of society'. But it

lies in the division of functions in the society rather than
in the division of rivals. And the 'needs' are not the need
for a public authority, but the need of one section for what
another can provide. *Given* the existence of state authority—
and the institution of public funds—the government can play
an important rôle in settling how these needs are satisfied.

An important rôle; but because power is of this kind it
can never be absolute. And if you show how the state operates with other forces, you may even make it look as though
state power were somehow a function of those forces or of
their organization, and not an independent force at all. But
although state power depends upon social organization—so
that you can almost say the power *is* the social organization—it can itself influence that organization and alter it.
When feudal societies became more bureaucratically organized, military power was separated from control of economy. The character of political power was changed, partly
because military and other state functionaries were dependent upon salaries from public funds. This had important
effects on military organization. But the influence of military power in other social affairs was changed too. On the
other hand, new forms of economy developed, independent
of military organization, and mobile wealth especially
became a power that had not been known before.[1] There
were new conceptions of property, new forms of control and
new social relations. The state did not initiate these
changes, but it had a good deal to do with them. They
would hardly have gone the way they did if the state had
not been there and taken on new functions. I do not mean
there would have been no social developments without it;
only they would have been different. The influences of
social forces on one another are different because they go
through political power. Which means that their influence—
the influence of wealth or of military forces, for instance—is
not entirely in their own hands. Just because political power
is not the power of any *one* force in the society, it has an
influence of its own.

[1] cf. G. Mosca, *The Ruling Class*, Eng. tr. p. 57.

This may be obscured it you think particularly of the party in power as the party 'of' some force or section of the society. Certainly you cannot understand political power without taking account of the party holding it. And in states which have not parties like those in Europe in modern times, it is still true, I suppose, that the holders of political office never rule alone; and you can often say that their rule is the rule of some more or less prevalent tendency. So it is always with some social policy, whether formulated or not, that political power is exercised. I doubt if the exercise of government is ever purely opportunist, although opportunism always enters in greater or less degree. And the party in power becomes decadent when it has nothing to offer.

But if any party exercises political power, then the character of its work is partly decided by that. It may be a party 'of' this section or that, and when it is not ruling it may voice their demands. But in ruling it will have to rely on other forces as well—without them it would not rule at all. And its legislative programme must be one that can be carried out. A legislative programme is not like a set of demands which a movement may push in order to win concessions *from* state power. In proportion as it has to take account of opposition, for instance, and to marshal support against it, the legislative policy must at least appear to be defensible on more general grounds. But the main point is that if you try to advance your aims by acquiring political power, this will influence the sort of aims you advance. Social movements may work to extend their influence without seeking political power at all, of course. And what they do in this way may be something political power could never do—because political power goes a different way.

The influence of political power is never just the influence of the party, or of those who support it.

It is not just that the party has acquired a new force. For in a way the party does not acquire this force at all, though it is able to act with it. This holds even when a revolutionary party destroys the existing state apparatus and institutes a new one. The party is now the government, it now has state power, and state action is something different from party action in this case also. The case may be different as long as considerable sections of the community do not recognize the new government—when they do not merely oppose its policies, but challenge its authority. It might be said that as long as that is so the government has not yet established itself. Anyway, it will depend upon coercion and not upon political power. But so far as it gets a 'de facto' recognition it will have political power, and the force which it exercises will not lie simply in its own strength and organization. It will control social forces, and its influence will lie in that control.

If political power is not the power of any one force in the community, that is a reason against calling the state a committee for managing the affairs of one class or movement. But it does not manage the affairs of the society as a whole either. Obviously, the management and organization of the bureaucracy is important, and the government's competence is sometimes judged by this. When the government takes over more public services and the control of industry, this may look like an extension of management—part of the centralization of the society's affairs. Certainly the new functions add to the government's tasks, and a large part of this increase is in the tasks of management. But ruling the society is not management of the society's affairs, for all that.

A society is not like a business concern, because there is nothing which is society's business. If you speak of managing the society's affairs—and if you go on to speak of running the society—you have to be arbitrary in what you select as its affairs, just as you would be in saying what its business was, or in deciding what is socially useful. And you would have to be arbitrary in calling any arrangement a 'co-ordination' of them. There may be some talk of 'legitimate demands', which reminds one of the 'legitimate aspirations' that are said to be considered in working out a 'just peace'. What happens in any case is that some policy is

6—WA

carried out, some sort of order is upheld as a compromise among the more powerful forces within the ruling body and outside it. You may call this good management in one sense of that expression, but it is not the management of society's affairs.

Here it may be important to distinguish between social movements and the 'functions' or 'activities' I spoke of earlier. In any of these, in the various branches of industry, in military and in police forces, or in religious or educational institutions, there are different ideas of carrying them on. There are different movements trying to influence the way the work goes and the policies that are followed. And similar tendencies in different fields may come together. The movement for a particular line in education may be linked with a movement in industry, and there may be similar opposition in both fields. So there are wider social conflicts and wider issues, including conflicting ideas about the interrelation of different activities.

For this reason you cannot speak of government control as co-ordination, simply. The co-ordination will always mean deciding for a particular policy. It will not be co-ordination among contending movements, and you cannot speak of co-ordination here.

These contending movements are in the nature of any social activity, and they belong as much to what we mean by society as any division of functions does. They certainly contribute to problems of government, and their conflicts may sometimes be called social problems. But they are not problems of organization. And the line the government takes to such social problems is not a solution of them.

What is 'solving the problems of coal production'? There are different ideas as to what these problems are. And such disagreement itself belongs to the 'problems of the coal industry'. But if the industry's problems include conflicts within it, they cannot all be removed—there is no solution anyway. The government may impose a settlement of a particular dispute, or the parties to it may reach a settlement themselves. But conflicting ideas about how coal mining should be carried on were not confined to that dispute. And this conflict goes on.

Such conflicts do not spring from misunderstandings, and it is senseless to 'seek a solution of them', whether in a special field or a wider one. No government policy can show the contending movements how to work together. They do 'live' together. And the laws that are enforced may favour one and make it difficult for the other. But they still have to find their own equilibrium or carry on their own fight. And no government plan arranges this.

If we ask whether the government has found the best solution of its problems, this may have sense, in reference to what the government is trying to do and the difficulties in the way of it. But it does not have sense to ask whether the government has found the best solution of the society's problems.

And even the question about the government's own problems may not be quite clear. Things may seem plain enough if you ask only how a declared policy can be carried out: how best to transfer key industries from private to public control, how to carry out a programme for schools and education, and so on. But it is not always easy, even for those in the government, to know whether the declared policy is what the government really wants. This is a kind of difficulty that may come up in any social movement. A movement tries to keep and develop a special way of working—in industry or in education or elsewhere. And it may be hard to decide whether by taking a particular line at this juncture, or making this new departure, they are going the way they want to go or not. Some of the difficulties are in knowing what will happen, e.g. will this course bring reactions of the sort we want to avoid? And for them a knowledge of sociology and economics may be important. But suppose you can make a fair estimate of the consequences, it may still be hard to decide whether the proposed course will really further the cause of the movement, even if those results do follow.

Many of the most important disputes within political

movements have been on questions of this kind. Compare the controversies between Lenin and Luxemburg, for instance; or between Bernstein and Kautsky. But even in movements that have not a political organization, the question 'Where are we going?' may come up in criticism of the character that the work is taking. In political movements especially, these questions are in fact not generally separated from questions of what is going to happen if the course is followed; and naturally so. But they are different questions all the same, and a different sort of wisdom is needed for them.

This is sometimes called political judgment. It is developed through working in the movement, and through experience of its relations with others. But this is not like the development of a skill. Political judgment is something different from sagacity in administration or brilliance in tactics. It appears often as a judgment of what is *important* or what is at stake in any conflict or discussion; seeing what the issues are. And although it will not grow in anyone who has neither worked in the movement nor thought about it, we do find 'sound political instincts' in persons who are less informed than some who show small sign of it.

Seeing what the issues are is also understanding the sort of conflicts that there are; or at least it leads to that. What is at stake, if it is not the immediate issue, is the persistence or decay of a movement of a particular character—a liberal movement in education, say—in its conflicts with other movements and in its need for new capacities as conditions change. Your perception of what the issues are decides what you are ready to fight for, and also how you will fight for it. The conflict, anyway, is a conflict between ways of working or ways of living. Where you cannot distinguish these (or if you cannot sense change of character—say the growth of servility—in a movement you have been working in), you may be blind to the conflict, or at any rate misplace it.

I doubt if there is any wisdom in ruling as distinct from wisdom in politics. Ruling does not get its character from the ambition or sense of responsibility of the rulers. (As if it were a matter of insight into affairs of state and of concern for the public welfare.) And it would not be on this that deeper political criticisms would be directed. For the holders of political office themselves act in a certain political or social current (or rather in various) which is the motive of the course they take, more fundamentally than their 'sense of responsibility' or 'public spirit' is. Their conception of affairs comes from this; and insight into affairs of state by another party would be different.

Political problems, for rulers as for others, lie largely with relations and conflicts among movements of different sorts. Because these are ways of working or ways of living, their conflicts may appear as struggles to maintain or establish one or another system of rights. Where the problem is only a problem of what will happen—whether a given proposal will be futile or not—the case is different. But that is not generally the main issue. And it is hard to see how there could be serious political conflicts if it were.

Burnham[1] would say, roughly: 'You may struggle for rights as much as you like; unless there is a separation and balance of social forces, such as wealth and military power and science and religion, your struggles will count for nothing at all'. But this seems almost to assume that those social forces do not have characters and policies. The idea seems to be that the various social forces seek to maintain power and influence, and perhaps independence, but nothing more. But independence of what? Surely of acting, of carrying on or pushing forward their affairs, and especially of the exercise of initiative. Burnham almost seems to think of them as physical forces without ideas. But the force of any opposition does depend partly in the consciousness with which it is exercised; or on the degree to which those who carry it are alive to the issue at stake. Otherwise the 'social force' is likely to grow servile and present no real opposition. This is as true of the so-called material forces, such as wealth and military power, as it is of any others. This is one reason why political science is often shaky in its predictions.

[1] In *The Machiaevellians*, especially Part VII.

Anyway, the degree of opposition in a society cannot be measured by the organization of the society, nor by the composition of its ruling class, if in that you consider only what functions or social forces enter into it.

It would be false, then, to think that the only antagonism between social forces is over who shall be boss. And it would be false to think that struggles for rights are of no real account to the serious student of social affairs.

It is true that historical study may deepen the understanding of political problems. And you can see much more if you have some knowledge of general laws and tendencies especially of economics. Mosca thinks the value of history for understanding politics is almost wholly in the generalizations it leads to. But I do not think that generalizations can really 'take us to the heart of political happenings', although you cannot go far without them. And they are not all that history can furnish. The question of 'what you can learn from history' is hard to answer, partly because it is not precise. Certainly it is philistine to reduce it to 'practical lessons'. And there is a difference between what I may call the extent and the depth of historical knowledge. Historical study may help, for instance, in the understanding of culture—though not by tracing general tendencies for the most part. And there is a different idea of why the period studied is important. Its importance is not so much in the light it throws on the general tendencies of institutions, but rather in the character of the work and achievements that can be studied there. For in that you may come to understand the difference between culture and commercialism, or between freedom and servility. This can often be seen through the study of other periods as it cannot by looking at what is done here and now. But it may deepen one's sense of the present issues.[1]

Learning from history in this way is comparable to the way in which you can learn from the lives of individuals; or from their work. It is not so much a question whether the

[1] cf. J. Anderson, *The Australasian Journal of Psychology and Philosophy*, December 1943, p. 172.

man made mistakes in his life or whether he didn't. But rather the way he made them. His seriousness or honesty, perhaps. Then his life and his inquiries are something you can learn from. 'Learn' in the sense in which people may speak loosely of 'what you can learn about life'.

This sort of understanding—as distinct from the knowledge of general laws—enters in *predictions* regarding political affairs as well. And again there is an analogy in the way in which you can make predictions about the life of an individual man. Laws and generalizations are important in both cases; but in a way they seem secondary. *Experience* is important; but not because it leads to general laws.

When predictions are made from the laws or tendencies of institutions, they are unreliable about as often as not. And I doubt if a greater wealth of knowledge can make them less so. There are various reasons for this. But one reason is connected with what Marxists call 'the subjective factor'. And the point is not that this is an undetermined agent, but that there are limits to the view you can get of it, or to your understanding of how it works. It is always hard to understand ways of living (and thinking and feeling) widely different from ours. This is familiar in the historical and anthropological studies of other cultures. And it is hard to foresee the growth or decline in the spirit of a movement, as it is to account for the flowering or decline of a culture. But these are not matters which the growing body of historical knowledge will do much to help, beyond making us more sensible of the difficulties.

If you rest with what you can predict from general tendencies you will hardly sense the issues that are being fought out. Perhaps no one ever does rest there. Anyway, a sense of what is going on does more for a decision on political problems than prediction does.

Political problems, as I speak of them here, are the problems which movements face, especially in relation to other movements and other policies. Perhaps there is no sharp line between political and other social problems. They are called political when they bear on the use of state power, or

at least when they touch wider social issues. To come to a
decision on a political problem is to come to terms with it in
some way. And that is a decision which movements reach in
their own ways, if at all. In any case, there is no *general* way
of deciding or dealing with social problems. If you said
there was, it would show a misconception of the problems
and of what could be meant by finding an answer to them.
And if there is no general way, there is no science of them,
or at any rate no science of their solution.

6

Politics and Justification

'What is the state?' may seem about as meaningless as 'What is the society we're living in?'

What are you *uncertain* about? What do you want to be told? Do you want to know the difference between state schools and private schools, perhaps? or between state grants and private endowments?

It is not a question like 'What is the gold standard?', where I really don't know what they're talking about and want to have it explained.

People have asked it—'What is the state?'—in political philosophy, when they were wondering, for example, what one's attitude towards the state should be; or wondering, perhaps, what sort of authority it is by which the state disposes of the lives and property of citizens.

It has often been part of a question about the individual's relation to the state. And this is not an easy expression either. The 'relation' seems to be an internal one; not like my relation to the park when I am in it. When I am not in the park, this will make no difference to the park or to me. But we cannot think of the state without thinking of individual citizens, nor vice versa. But neither is 'the relation of the individual to the state' at all like 'the relation of the individual wolf to the pack' or 'the relation of the individual to the crowd'. These could be understood as quasi-physical relations, and the relation of the individual to the state is not that. It has rather to be studied, apparently, in terms of obligations. I suppose this is one of the reasons why seventeenth and eighteenth-century writers placed such emphasis upon the notion of social contract.

But neither is it simply a question regarding 'a man's duties to other men'; it is not (or not primarily) a question about morality. To say, for instance, 'The principles discussed in political philosophy involve value judgments' hardly takes us beyond the threshold. How are they different from moral principles, then?

We may try to clarify the conception 'a man's duties to other individuals'—to explain our use of this expression, what we mean by it. And we'd probably call this a discussion in moral philosophy. But if we try to explain to ourselves the meaning of 'a man's duties to the community (or society)' this will be in many ways a different sort of discussion.

The phrase, 'an individual's duties to the community', might refer to civil or legal duties, such as my duty to pay taxes, my duty to undertake jury service if called upon, my duty to report a theft or other crime I may have witnessed, etc. On the other hand it might mean 'moral duties to the community', which need not coincide with any legal duties, and may even, in special circumstances, conflict with legal duties. This conception seems the more interesting of the two. It is also much harder to make clear; as we see at once when we try to give appropriate examples of it.

People sometimes say 'duties to society' and sometimes 'duties to others'—almost as though there were no difference. But if we do run them together, we have confused *both* conceptions. My duties to others are generally duties to *particular* people: members of my family, my friends, students I have taught, someone I've employed. . . .

If we spoke of 'love or charity towards all men', and if this 'all' meant not simply 'without discrimination, no matter who the man may be' but is somehow meant to *include* everybody, as when a mother is said to love all her children—then perhaps this would have sense in the case of a few great saints (I do not know); but it would *not* mean 'charity towards society'. And similarly for any 'duties towards all men'.

'An individual's duties to the community.' (Suppose I feel it my duty to speak out on some issue of national importance; perhaps the admission or exclusion of immigrants of other races.)

Can we speak in a similar way of the community's duties towards individuals? So that the *community* could be blamed for neglect of them? That would be a queer sense of 'blame'. When it was said 'We are all to blame for the rise of Hitler', this meant 'each *one* of us is to blame'. The blame is borne by each individual. If I say 'the alarming rise in juvenile delinquency shows that there is something wrong with our society'—this is different. I am not blaming any individual, nor saying that everyone is to blame.

Or again: 'There is something wrong with a society in which men are afraid to criticize the government'.

Or: 'There is something wrong with any society in which there is nothing like the right of *habeas corpus*'.

Obviously this does not mean that there is something wrong with each individual in such a society. But is there any conception of blame or of dereliction of duty at all involved here?

Here we are concerned with judgments like 'There is something wrong where there is no right of *habeas corpus*' rather than with 'There is something wrong with a society showing so rapid a rise in juvenile delinquency'. Partly because it has to do directly with state and individual.

When a man makes such a judgment, this is not just an arbitrary statement of opinion. If we ask him why he says it, he may go over the main events leading up to the Habeas Corpus Act; he may remind us of the difference which this made to the character of British government and to the position of the judiciary, and so on. It may be clear that he feels deeply about these events. And perhaps in the end we shall agree with him about *habeas corpus*.

If we had put our question in the form, 'You say there is something wrong with a society where there is no such right; well, *what's* wrong? What does it mean to say that the society has something wrong with it?'—he might answer in the same way: speaking of what happened before the Act which led men to press for it, then considering the difference it made.

We had asked him 'Why?'. And I think we should say he has given his reasons for thinking *habeas corpus* important—so far as it is possible to talk of reasons in questions of this kind.

If you and I both want to preserve and extend the liberties that are allowed in our society, we may discuss whether, say, proportional representation would make the regime more liberal or less so. Ought one to work for the introduction of PR, or would one be justified in opposing it? Here we know in a general way the kind of issues that would be raised. And we know what it would mean to say that the one side or the other had proved its case.

But consider: 'Are we justified in wanting to preserve and promote liberty?' How could there be a discussion of *that*?

(Someone might claim that in special circumstances—a war or a plague—liberty would have to be sacrificed until the danger was past. And others might dispute this. But this does not affect the case I am considering.)

Some feel that the preservation of liberty is more important than anything else in public affairs, and they find it hard to understand how anyone can think it is not. Others think liberty an expendable luxury compared with the need for order and strong government.

Each party might bring objections to what the other was saying and ask how he would answer that. But it is unlikely that one or the other will recognize 'something still more ultimate and important than liberty' or 'something more ultimate and more important than order'. As it were something on which the *importance* of liberty rests. For the man devoted to liberty, there is nothing which *makes* liberty important. And he has no reason for his devotion.

If a man is determined to fight for liberty (for the furtherance of liberty in this society)—then fine.

But if he says he is determined to fight for liberty *for the reason that* . . . —then I lose interest.

And similarly if he is determined to fight for the achievement of communism.

It is not as though 'there is something *about* a liberal society from which anyone can see that liberty is important'. No doubt there would be differences between a liberal society and an authoritarian one; different institutions (free and frequent elections, limitations on police powers: 'inviolability of the domicile', etc.) and different methods of enforcing them. And I might describe these. I might emphasize that in the authoritarian society 'people are never allowed to' do this and that; and I might call this tyranny— although this is no longer pure description. The man devoted to order and strong government might answer that he does not find tyranny so very objectionable; things like insecurity, uncertainty, time wasting disputes, the want of any clear regularity in the life of the community, not knowing what we can expect—these are greater evils for the mass of the people than any tyranny would be. And so on. It is not that he and I understand something different by 'liberty'. We may agree on that. In other words, if I do care about liberty, then I shall want to defend the freedom of the press, the inviolability of the domicile, etc. We might even say that caring about liberty *means*, inter alia, wanting to defend these institutions and practices. But then we should add that I do not have any *reason* for wanting to defend them.

7

'Responsibility to Society'

I distrust the phrase 'responsibility to society' because it suggests that society expects certain things of us; or of me.

It goes together sometimes with a reference to 'the good of society'; and to doing things 'in the interests of society'. And it sometimes goes with the condemnation of certain actions as 'anti-social'.

These phrases are so confused, and they breed so much confusion, that I prefer to avoid them. It is very likely that I assume too readily that any use of 'responsibility to society' is confused, before I have taken pains to examine it in this or that particular case.

I thought the best of R.'s examples was that of the directors or managers of a factory, who arrange for the factory waste to be discharged into a river, so that the river is polluted. I agree that such people might be said to show want of responsibility, and perhaps that they would be said to be acting irresponsibly. R. suggested that they might reply that they were showing concern for their workers—their responsibility was to their workers. And he thought that we might answer that they had not only a responsibility to their workers but also a responsibility to society. And he said we should mean by this that they should bear in mind the interests of people—any people—who might want to use the river.

I should agree with this latter way of putting their responsibility or with this interpretation of what were meant by saying that they had acted irresponsibly. I do not think it makes anything clearer to call this 'responsibility to society'. And I cannot see why anyone should want to call it that. I *think* the reason is that this way of putting it— 'responsibility to society'—seems to make the rebuke much sterner and much more grave. As though 'society', i.e. the unknown people who might want to use the river, had a much more overriding claim for consideration than the employees of the factory had. And this seems to me humbug.

I do not know how old the term 'society' in this sense is. But I suspect that it is relatively new. I believe the term 'civilization' was never used before the seventeenth century. (I suppose they had not seen the importance of saving it.) And I guess that 'society' is later than that. Anyway, at the present time, it has become *loaded* with emotional meanings and suggestions of importance.

For example: society is everyone, and so the good of society is the good of everyone. And the highest morality (i.e. the morality which is intoned by government speakers) is the consideration of the good of all. Of each and everyone of us (it is the cadence of this phrase that counts).

Whenever you do anything for the good of society, you are being *entirely* unselfish. As, for example, in socialism and in social service.

The same thing holds for 'the general interest'. Suppose R. had said that the factory management ought to have considered the general interest, and not just the interest of the workers in that factory. What this means is that they ought to have considered anyone who might want to use the river. Very good.

But then the 'general interest' is taken to be 'the interest of *everyone*'. And so . . . Well if you put *any* interest above the general interest, then you are following a selfish interest, a sectional interest, and so on.

Whereas in fact there *is* no general interest. I mean: there is no sense in speaking of some one thing (or set of things) or some one social arrangement, which everyone wants. Nor that there is any which everyone could be induced to want—by having it shown that such an arrangement would further the aims which he *does* have.

What is called 'the general interest' is an arrangement which the speaker, perhaps sincerely, thinks would be *best* for everyone. But in fact any such arrangement will place restrictions on the activities of certain people. And it is an arbitrary assumption that it is to the advantage of these people to accept the arrangements, instead of fighting things out on their own.

We should distrust any statement about what is 'in the interests of education', if the speaker had no experience of educational work himself. And this holds generally of activities and movements. There is no one who is qualified to speak on behalf of all. And it is humbug for anyone to advocate something 'in the interests of all'.

To say that everyone has a responsibility to society may be taken to mean that everyone ought to show a regard for the interests of society. And in this case I think there is confusion, and often dishonesty. There is dishonesty, because this is generally a way of advocating certain particular interests—perhaps the maintenance of 'public order', a general rise in the standard of living (i.e. in money incomes or in real incomes)—even though various people or various sections in society would say that these things are less important than other things or other activities to which they are devoted. It will not do to say that these people are setting their own interests against the interests of society. They are setting their own interests against the interests of those who are opposed to them; that is all.

Nor can it be said that 'society could not go on' if people insisted on pressing sectional interests. That is how society does go on.

People often say in a general way that someone has acted irresponsibly. Someone said this recently about school-girls who have become pregnant. And we might say that picnickers had acted irresponsibly if they had gone away and left a fire smouldering near to dry grass and bushes.

This means that they acted without regard for the consequences of what they were doing. And it is generally suggested that a reasonable person would have done otherwise: where 'a reasonable person' is a kind of standard. 'It is *not too much to ask*' of any person of normal intelligence, that he reflect on the danger of leaving a fire smouldering there—especially in view of the publicity that has been given to such things, etc. . . . (I do not think quite the same sort of argument can be applied to the pregnant schoolgirls.)

There are thousands of such examples. It might be said that someone had acted in a way that was a danger to public health by allowing unsanitary conditions to develop on his farm or in his garden. Perhaps R. would say that the preservation of public health is in the interests of everyone. But not every *measure* to preserve public health is in the interests of everyone.

'Public health' itself is often a pretty vague notion. (Coughs and sneezes spread diseases: trap the germs in your handkerchief. I think that is admirable advice. Many people cannot be bothered, and I think they act irresponsibly. But I should not say that they had failed in their responsibility to society. I should never ask anybody to consider society if I were trying to get him to stop coughing and sneezing all over people. I should try to get him to consider the people he is coughing over.)

The women who complain about the emptiness of their lives when they have young children, may have good ground for complaint. I did not want to question this. I am unclear about what the complaint generally is. And prima facie it seems strange that this should be a 'new situation'. But the complaint may amount to saying that there is something wrong with the institution of marriage and the family. I should not wish to quarrel with this, although it is fairly obvious that any remedy will bring some disadvantages (e.g. for the children if not for the mothers), and women will probably disagree as to which disadvantages are the most grave. But for all that, I can sympathize with the feeling that 'having a family ought not to be like this'; and even with the feeling that 'it surely *need* not be like this'.

I did think there was something wrong in the statement that 'society got us into this, so it is up to society to get us out'.

I think if I were such a woman, I should welcome the help of almost anyone except Society. And if Society came messing around I should say, 'Listen, you got us into this: now get the hell out.'

But I am not such a woman.

In the field of international politics, a statesman is said to be looking after the interests of his country (and he may do this well or ill). This may have given rise to the conception of what is 'in the national interest'; although I think this is a later notion, and it is generally more vague and more slippery.

Perhaps the idea of 'the interests of society' is a further derivative still. It is much harder to find any definite or legitimate use for it.

8

'Natural Law' and Reasons in Ethics

I do not understand the relation between lex naturalis and lex divina in St. Thomas. But I have supposed that he spoke, sometimes anyway, of the lex naturalis as a law which men could know by the lumen naturale—for the knowledge or understanding of which we do not need the lumen divinum. And I thought Fr. R. wanted to say that *because* it is a law of reason, therefore it can be known and understood by all men. (And conversely: If you cannot understand or recognize it, then you are not a man. Here 'man' is clearly not a biological term, but an expression of *value*. Cf. 'be a man!' etc. But it is *also* an expression of value when he speaks of 'reflexion on the nature of man'. And writers might—and do—differ on 'what it means to be a man'. This difference cannot be settled by any discussion on biology. If you say it can be settled at all, does this mean that there is some *further* natural law, found by reflexion on . . . ? regressus ad inf.

It was a kindred use—as an expression of value—when Renaissance writers spoke of 'human dignity' or 'the dignity of man'.)

This might mean: a man ought to be able to see (understand) that a practice—say contraception—is contrary to nature, even though he did not understand that it was forbidden by God. He ought to be able to see this, because there are *reasons* which can make it plain to him—reasons which he can understand without any reference to the will of God. But then what is the force of: *see that it is contrary to nature*? Does this mean (1) see that there *are* reasons for condemning it? or (2) see that 'being contrary to nature' is a reason for condemning it?

If 'it is contrary to nature' *means* 'there is a "natural" reason for condemning it'—then the reason in question cannot be: *that* it is contrary to nature.

I think Fr. R. was suggesting:

'The natural law is what makes ethical reasons into ethical reasons.'

But what does this tell us? I might ask: 'What do you call an "ethical reason"?'; or 'How do you distinguish sound from unsound reasons in ethical discussions?' It would be interesting, but difficult, to try to answer this by considering a lot of examples, seeing where there are common features, where there are important differences and so on; noticing also circumstances in which you would say that 'this is not an ethical reason at all' (i.e. it is irrelevant to the ethical question). If Fr. R. or anyone else could help me by giving examples and discussing them, I should be grateful. But what help is it simply to say: 'There is something which makes an ethical reason into an ethical reason'?

Fr. R. might answer: 'It says that all ethical reasons have something in common. All can be measured against one another. And so there is a common basis for discussion—*wherever* ethical reasons are offered'. But there is something begging question here. The statement 'All ethical reasons have something in common' *might* be trivial—might mean no more than 'they are all ethical reasons'. We can point to analogies in the way in which reasons are used in one situation and in another, and if I ask you 'Would you call that an ethical reason?', you say 'Of course'. But from:

'They have something in common—otherwise we should not call them ethical reasons', you cannot pass to:

'Wherever ethical reasons are offered, there must be a common basis for discussion.'

Or again: from 'They have something in common', you cannot conclude:

'There is one reason which is *always* being offered, or implied, wherever an ethical reason is offered.'

This is not only unwarranted; it is not even plausible at all. Because, for instance, if you tried to formulate any such reason, it would be so empty that it could not be a reason for anything.

(When Fr. R. argues in this way, he *is* confusing *form of reasoning* and *premiss*—in spite of the fact that he recognizes the confusion in St. Thomas. Confer: 'You would never consider reasons for making a moral decision, unless you recognized that there is a difference between good and evil. Therefore: "That there is a difference between good and evil" is always among your reasons for making the moral decision which you do.' But this is not the chief point of my disagreement with him.)

Why do people emphasize 'universality', when they are speaking of ethical judgments? 'universal validity', 'binding on all men', etc.?

(1) They feel that this universality shows that the judgment is not just a private prejudice.

(2) They feel that, if an obligation is really binding, then it must be so on account of something more important than the particular circumstances. So it has been said that the ethical judgment '*goes beyond* all circumstances'. And similarly: when you praise or condemn a man for what he has done, your praise or condemnation has a significance which is not *confined* to these particular circumstances and this particular time. (If I have put the motor together wrongly, I shall have to take it apart and do it over again. But if you have treated your friend in a despicable way, then there is no 'going back and doing it over again without that fault'.)

But: To say that a moral judgment 'goes beyond particular circumstances', does not mean that it is *based* on anything.

The idea of *foundations for ethics* (or: foundations for jurisprudence): 'What makes ethical reasons into ethical reasons'. Perhaps: 'so that ethical discussions are not just empty—there is something real in it'. This is similar to the idea of *foundations for logic* or *foundations for mathematics*.

And to say that it makes ethical judgments into something real, is the same as saying that they are not just *arbitrary*.

But:

either the foundations are some pronouncement which is *not* ethical—and then no judgment of value follows from them;

or they *are* a judgment of value (or ethical judgment): and then there *can* be ethical judgments which need no foundations to '*make*' them ethical judgments.

What keeps the *foundations*—the law of nature—from being 'arbitrary'? Or what is *ethical* (or 'practical') about the law of nature?

Some people dislike the thought that 'there are many who would judge differently, or decide differently, on this moral issue'. But why should this disturb them?

I saw no reason to think that whenever people disagree on a moral issue, it must be *possible* for them to reach agreement. This does not mean that it is *never* possible for them to reach agreement (though some hearers took it to mean this). But often it is not; and I said that this did not disturb me. This confused people. They thought I was saying that any condemnation of a man's action ('That was a foul thing to do') is just an explanation of 'how I see it'; and that of course others may see it in a different way 'which is just as good'. As though I had said there are no real disagreements on moral questions. Or: as though I do not *deny* what another man says when (e.g.) he praises the action which I condemn.

It is always hard to see how people can mistake your meaning so completely. But I should have spoken more plainly.

Fr. R. spoke of 'getting at the truth' on a moral question and of 'getting at the truth regarding the right system of ethics'. I would repeat that ' "p" is true' adds nothing to 'p'. And 'That system of ethics is false' is a *denial*. It expresses my rejection of that system of ethics. That way of speaking—'getting at the truth'—or: 'arriving at the truth': as though there were something which would show when we had arrived—this is taken over from investigations into matters of fact; and perhaps to some extent from discussions of problems in mathematics. 'Perhaps we shall never know the truth regarding who was responsible for this crime.' I heard a County court judge tell Counsel not to cut short the examination of a witness, adding: 'I want to get to the bottom of this'. But it shows confusion if you speak this way about moral questions.

Of course there are *discussions* on moral questions. And I may say, 'I wish to God I could see what I ought to do', or 'I wish I knew whether the decision I have taken was right'. But this does not mean that in some sense the answer is already settled (as in the case of the crime committed) and that my difficulty is to *find* it. My trouble is that I have to *decide*. I may speak of 'knowing' in this connexion—'I know that this is the only thing for me to do'. But if you speak of this as 'reaching the truth', then this suggests that other people ought to be able to see it in the same way as I do: just as a mathematician may be able to show others the truth of the solution he has found. Whereas in many— perhaps most—questions of morals the decision has to come from me (from the man who faces it); and *whatever the rôle of reasons, etc., may be, they are never conclusive in the way the steps of a mathematical proof are,* nor in the way in which material evidence of guilt in connexion with a crime may be. I know that Fr. R. did refer to Aristotle's remark about the contingency of the conclusions of practical reason. But sometimes he spoke as though he had forgotten it. And anyway, I do not think Aristotle weighed sufficiently the question of what a 'reason' for a decision is: the point that what I would regard as a reason, might not be a reason for you—might not function as a reason in your decisions. This is not trivial, and you cannot brush it off by murmuring 'relativism'. It is bound up with the whole point that the decision has to come from the person involved. Even the *problem* is hardly ever the same from one person to another. And what makes it the problem it is for me are the reasons which weigh with me in the one direction and in the other. If in the face of these reasons I conclude that I ought to give up my job, another man considering the same reasons might conclude differently. Perhaps I shall think that what he has decided to do is wrong. But I might *not* think this. It was his decision, and—in an important sense—it was his problem. When I decide that this is the only thing for me to do, I am *not* saying that it would be the only thing for any man in just these circumstances to do.

And why should anyone think that this showed my conviction that I can do nothing else must have been half-hearted?

If I do think that the man who decided differently was wrong, I could not speak of *proving* he was wrong. That has no sense. This does not mean that I am uncertain, or that I cannot say definitely that he *is* wrong.

Someone says: 'But if you cannot prove it, then you may be wrong yourself; and you may be wrong when you say that *he* is'. Well, what does this show? Sometimes I see afterwards that I *have* been wrong. But how do I see this? Not by any conclusive proof of the universal practical reason. I see it by being convinced that I ought *not* to have done this: i.e. once again by being sure. 'We could never find out that we have made mistakes, unless we sometimes made no mistakes.' When you tell me that I am wrong, then you are not uttering a logical absurdity: what you are saying makes sense, and I can understand it. In fact, I should not have had the trouble in *coming* to my decision otherwise. So I admit that my decision 'may be wrong', if this is all that is meant. But this does not mean that I must say 'And yet I know I may be wrong'—as though I were hesitant or wavering. Often enough I am hesitant; but not on *these* grounds.

Fr. R. emphasized the importance of *responsibility* in connexion with moral decisions. Well, exactly.

9

On Knowing the Difference Between Right and Wrong

H. wanted to discuss various versions of 'moral nihilism' and to ask whether they were incoherent or not. He said that the expression 'to opt out of morality' was obscure enough to merit philosophical discussion. But just where does the obscurity of it lie, and why is it that 'this expression is much used at the present time'—why is it that people *do* speak in this way? (I had not realized that they do.)

Philosophers often speak of 'morality'—as though it were plain what is meant by this. It seems that there are those who care about morality, and there are those who wish to opt out of morality—almost as though 'morality' were a term comparable to 'military service' or 'membership of the National Union of Railwaymen'. But there are various people who might be said to care about morality, although they (*a*) use the term in very different ways, and (*b*) have very different ways of showing that they 'care'.

e.g.: I believe there is a body called The Church of England Moral Welfare Council (or some name similar to that). I once heard a report of an interview between one of their local committees and an unmarried girl who was pregnant and who had got into their clutches, I suppose, because she was in a very distressed state and perhaps seeking admission to a Home for her confinement. The line of the moral woman in the chair was: 'Do you know you can be locked up if you go on like this? Do you want to be locked up?' etc. I imagine the Morality of these people could be described pretty definitely. (In fact H.'s description of morality as 'a system of restraints and initiatives', in which a concern for other people is central would fit the mores of the Moral Welfare Council like a glove, although I know this was not what he had in mind.) And it might be clear enough what someone meant if he said he would opt out of morality, as they speak of it; or if he said 'to hell with that'.

These people have a large family of cousins—those who want to clean up TV, etc., etc.

H. would say that the expression 'to hell with that' is not an expression of moral nihilism, as he wants to consider it, but rather a judgment of value; or at least that it often is so. I think the activities of those moral enthusiasts are foul and filthy; and in academic discussions this would be called a moral judgment on them. But if one is to emphasize this, then one should discuss what *this* moral judgment has in common with the moral judgments of the Moral Welfare Council: how is it related to them and how does it differ from them? Suppose I *dispute* the remark that 'their activities are foul and filthy' is a moral judgment—what would be said to show that it *is*? I think the differences are just as marked and just as important as the similarities. And if you offered reasons for saying that both are forms of moral judgment, I think there are reasons just as strong for saying they are not.

On the other hand, if H. had referred to both sorts of comment as—e.g. and along with others—*examples* of the general sort of comment and criticism he was wanting to discuss, then it would be all right. We should have taken this as an introductory explanation, the sense of which would become clearer in the course of his paper. We should have expected him to take account of the differences as well as the analogies, but there *are* certain analogies, and there may be reasons (sometimes, but not always) for considering the two sorts of comment together.

Once I was speaking to an elderly man about a younger man who had got himself into a mess. The older man seemed to think it was the young man's own fault, and that it was the people harmed by him who were to be pitied. I did not dispute this, but I went on to explain more in detail what his situation was. At one point the older man asked with sarcasm, 'So he *does* know the difference between right and wrong, does he?'

When a man says that, there is sometimes a suggestion that if the fellow has shown that he does not even know the difference between right and wrong, then he deserves no mercy. On the other hand, someone might say it to me—or ask it of me—in order to pull me up: like asking 'do you realize what you are doing?' Perhaps this would be the more general use of it. If you said of someone who was unscrupulous in a big way, say of Hitler, or of Archelaos in the *Gorgias*, 'He does not seem to know the difference between right and wrong'—people would think you were trying to be funny: it would sound like a stage caricature of a nurse maid. We should want to ask, 'What's that got to do with it?'

Are there certain people of whom it would be said that they do not know the difference between right and wrong? And if so, what is being said? What is it that they do not know?

(I think I have heard so-called 'psychopaths' described in this way, but I have never seen just how it fits. There are people who are completely unmoved by the harm they have done to other people—even to people who have done nothing to them—but who have an exaggerated sense of the wrong which other people have done to *them*. I believe I have heard such people called 'psychopaths'—and certainly they are *dangerous*—but it is queer to say they have no sense of right and wrong and at the same time that they have a strong sense that they themselves are victims of injustice.)

What I want to ask is whether there is something you can call 'knowing the difference between right and wrong'

77475

which is the same, no matter what the character of the judgments or the decisions—no matter whether you think that initiative and enterprise, putting your talents to profitable use, is the most important thing, or whether you think that humility and poverty is the most important thing, etc., etc. I get the impression sometimes that Plato or Socrates thought that we could speak of knowing the distinction between the *forms* of justice and of injustice (if he does speak of a form of injustice) as something which is the same even where the laws and the standards of praise and blame: i.e. the special sorts of action which are praised and the special sorts of action for which men are blamed or punished, may be very different and almost antithetical. (Suppose a society in which acquiring private property is a capital offence and murder is not a very serious offence. Or perhaps: the 'moralities' of certain anarchists and those of militarists.) I doubt if Plato would have said this in the later part of his life. But those who speak nowadays of 'knowing the difference between right and wrong' make me wonder sometimes if they are thinking along the same lines. And the trouble is that I do not know what these lines are.

I feel like asking: 'Well, what *is* the difference between right and wrong?'

I suppose the only answer that could be given would have to be something on the lines of Socrates's answer to Glaucon in the *Republic*, when Glaucon asked him to 'tell us what *you* think "the good" is?'

It is just the sort of question you cannot answer.

If you asked me whether I knew the difference between right and wrong—I should wonder what you were getting at. (I hope I should never reply, 'Of course I do!')

If I understand him, H. would discuss someone who 'knows the meaning of right and wrong, but yet. . . .' But yet what?

Sometimes H. seemed to be speaking of someone who was familiar with the sorts of things which most people would *call* right or wrong: the sorts of actions which are in accordance with the accepted moral standards of the community, and the sorts of action which are not. A man might know this, just as he might know which works of music were generally praised by musical people, or which pictures were regarded as the best pictures ('the 100 best pictures'), although as far as he was concerned they could change places with the pictures which are generally called atrocious. But this will not really cover the sort of man or the sort of attitude which he wanted to discuss.

In one sense certain of the Stoic and the Epicurean and the early Christian communities were 'opting out' of morality; just as certain of the Beatniks are.

It always muddles the discussion when someone speaks as though there were some all embracing morality—some *general* moral principle or ultimate standard, of which the standards the people of these various communities recognize are so many different expressions. I can see no good reason for saying this, and I think it is generally confusing. (For one thing, if you leave it as I have just stated it, then it looks as though 'recognizing standards' were the same sort of 'activity' or 'attitude' in the early Christian and in the Beatnik—which is blatantly false.)

So if someone tries: 'The Stoics and Cynics were opting out of the accepted morality of the Roman burghers—but they were not opting out of *Morality*'—I can only say that I am not impressed. I do not say that someone who said this would not have anything which could be discussed. But he has not made it clear what this is. Part of what he means, I suppose, is that the reaction of the Stoic or the Beatnik is not simply *negative*: he is making a positive move in another direction. I agree that this is important. But can 'repudiating morality' be understood in some way which does not include this? or is this part of what we should *mean* by repudiating morality?

What Kierkegaard called 'the aesthetic view of life' was still a view of life. But he did not call it *ethical* on that account.

One reason why H.'s references to 'moral nihilism' were unclear:

He seems to think of the 'nihilist' as a disputant or a sceptic in *moral philosophy*.

When H. classifies the different positions which the nihilist might take up 'towards morals', he means, apparently, towards *discussions* of morals. And H. did not give any examples of discussions of morals which were *practical*. He *seemed* to be speaking of discussions of what morality *is*: the kind of 'validity' it has, and so on.

Hence the feeling (*my* feeling, anyway) that the 'nihilist' is a philosophical construction: a personification of certain objections of which a moral philosopher thinks he should take account if he is to 'look at every side of the question'.

If a man be really beset by moral difficulties, then I imagine he would want particularly to avoid these philosophical discussions. ('Don't play with the difficulties in people's lives.')

10

'What are Moral Statements Like?'

If anyone does ask 'What *are* moral statements like?', I should think one ought to begin by giving examples of them. But often writers on ethics do not do this. You mention 'Honesty is good'. I cannot remember ever hearing anyone say this, unless it be in a philosophical discussion. And I cannot imagine just the circumstances under which anyone *would* say it. I remember once when someone did say very seriously, 'Well, thanks for the honesty; that's much better than philosophy'. But of course, if you consider an example of this sort the question whether the goodness is a quality like redness would hardly arise.

Again, I can remember a remark in the course of a biography. The writer quotes a poem which was written by the wife of one of the people he was writing about. And then he says, 'Not a good poem. But a good woman. That often happens.'

But the examples for which I would look especially would be examples of moral problems. I mean problems by which people are faced when they may feel like saying 'I wish to God I knew what I ought to do'. Treatises on ethics sometimes talk about 'conflicts of duties'. But that phraseology is already making the matter pretty artificial, I think.

I should want to bring out something of the *kind* of importance which moral problems have. I might try to show how they are unlike problems regarding health or sickness, for instance. But more especially, I should try to show how they are unlike problems relating to success or failure in one's vocation (although of course such questions run into one another often). 'If I cannot find some answer, I cannot carry on in business at all.' 'If I cannot find some way out, I shall have to give up teaching.' But then what about the moral problem? 'If I cannot find some way . . .' What is the urgency here?

'I shall never be any better in music, I can see now that I shall never be a musician.' 'Well, you'll have to take up something else.'

But: 'I just never get any better (morally). With every failure, I have found the courage to go on only with the thought that by trying I shall gradually get better. And I have only to look at the record now, to know that I never shall.' Well? Tell him to take up something else?

'If you're not a first rate teacher, then you'll just have to learn to live with the fact that you are a second rate or a third rate teacher.'

'If you find that you just are never going to be decent, even to the people that you love, then you'll just have to . . .' Hell.

In what situations does one use moral expressions? What sort of questions is one trying to answer? Are you wondering how to *describe* something?

When you raise the question 'What are moral statements like?', you seem to be asking what *other* statements they are like—how we ought to class them: Are we describing or ejaculating?—and this seems to me the wrong way to begin. It seems to assume that they must be a special case of some other class of statement. Whereas I want to say, 'Never mind that. When and where do you find them? Under what circumstances do you know you have to do with moral statements? And what sort of questions, what sort of problems, what sort of worries and what sort of answers do they call forth? Suppose you disagree with somebody in the course of a moral statement. What would be an example of this? And what sort of issue would it be? i.e. what sort of considerations would it depend on?'

If you start by amalgamating them with some other sort of statement, it is likely that you will never see what they are like.

Of course, it is the analogies which there are between the statements made in moral discussions and statements made in other circumstances—it is this which gives rise to part of your problem.

You take something like, 'Granting that it is a fact that honesty is good, why should I bother about it?'

Contrast: (1) 'It is a fact that honesty is good';
         (2) 'I agree that—or I see that—honesty is good.'

If someone said (2) and then went on '. . . but I don't see why I should pay any regard to it', you would not think he was talking good sense. You might ask about the 'why I *should* pay . . .': What is it that you don't see? What kind of reason are you looking for?

This has analogies with the more general question about 'a reason for believing something' and again with 'a reason for doing something'. I will return to this.

Perhaps some would fear to put it in form (2) ('I see that honesty is good') because they fear 'subjectivism'. But of course the statement does not mean 'I *like* honesty', as though it were like saying 'I like someone who is keen on sports'. (In certain contexts 'I like honesty' may be used as a genuine expression of moral judgment, but then it is not just an expression of personal taste.) Someone who says 'I see that honesty is good' may have thought a lot about the distinction of good and evil, or right and wrong, in various cases. He is not just saying how he *happens* to feel. ('I feel like taking a walk.' 'I feel like being honest.')

A follower of Anderson might say, 'But the important question, or the only relevant question, is not whether you *see* that honesty is good, but whether it is good'. I think this is just stupid.

8—WA * *

There are obvious analogies in aesthetics. If someone
says 'I think Beethoven's Third Symphony is a wonderful
thing', this is not like 'I adore vanilla ice cream'. Think of
the ways you might compare the symphony with other
works of music, or perhaps with works of literature or of
architecture. If I told you, 'I have never been able to understand it; I wish you could explain to me a little'—you
might be able to say certain things about it: both about its
structure, and about its 'ideas'. All of this would belong to
your reasons for saying that it is a wonderful thing. And
nothing of the sort would have any sense in connexion with
the vanilla ice.

('It is just a fact that the symphony is wonderful;
whether anyone recognizes it or not.' This would be silly.)

Similarly, I might say 'I don't think honesty is as important as you make it out to be' (which would not mean 'I am
not so very fond of it'). Then I should probably go on to
consider the relation of honesty to other things that people
do; to the situations in which it is shown or is wanting, and
so on. I am not telling you something about *my state of
mind* when I say that I feel this way about honesty.

On the other hand, if I had said 'I don't think that
smoking is as dangerous as the doctors make it out to be',
this would have been a different sort of statement. And we
could show this, once more, by considering the reasons that
could be offered for it; or—as we might say in connexion
with the dangers of smoking—by considering the way in
which the statement could be verified.

It is true that in connexion with *both* kinds of statement
I am suggesting that the other man is making a mistake.
And it is often important to emphasize that one can make
mistakes in moral judgments and that one can learn, e.g.: 'I
can see the depth and the importance of humility now,
although for a long time I could not. I thought it was just
masochism'.

But it is a confusion to suppose that whenever you
speak of making a mistake you mean something like a
mistake in physics or in medicine or in a newspaper report.

Certainly, both there and in connexion with moral judgment it means that you can be mistaken or can be wrong.
(But keep from adding, '... i.e. that the facts are otherwise'. This only confuses matters.) Then consider how you
came to say that you were wrong. Or the kind of reasons
you might give for saying that someone else is wrong in his
judgment, say, about suicide. This will show you what you
mean by 'mistakes' in this kind of case.

(And of course, if you can be wrong, then you cannot say
that each man's opinions are true for him while he holds
them.)

I expect your trouble is partly in thinking of someone who does not know what is meant by 'ought' and
'good' and the many other expressions that go with these
(moral philosophers have not helped matters by concentrat-
ing on those two). Maybe a man could be familiar with the
common use of these terms—he may know that people say
it is good to be generous, and that it is wrong to think only
of yourself, and so on. He could repeat such statements as
he might repeat other things that are generally said. And
yet they might mean nothing to him—just as 'nuclear
fission' or 'chain reaction' or 'polarization' might mean
nothing to him. Although he hears them all the time. (I am
blind even to the sense of less technical expressions. I never
know what is meant by 'He remarked dryly' or 'He smiled
wryly'.) You might almost want to say that he knows the
ethical expressions from without but not from within.

I think this raises the question of how people do learn to
understand moral expressions. And the discussion of this
would take me longer than I can try to go now. You might
give a fairly simple account of some of the first stages of
such learning (and these are important). In the later
stages—learning the uses of these expressions in their connexions with more serious problems—it would be more
complicated.

At no stage would this be a causal account. Nor is it
anything like sociology. Ayer seems to have gone muddled
about this.

At any rate, children *do* learn to understand these expressions. And obviously they do not learn what 'good' means in anything *like* the way in which they learn what 'red' means. They learn to understand what adults mean in using moral expressions; and they understand that adults are not just speaking about—describing—'what all people do', or anything of that sort. They learn to ask questions in connexion with such remarks; and—more important—they learn to answer questions. They learn to use such expressions themselves.

They learn all this, of course, in connexion with praise and blame, admiration and contempt.

And I think they learn to use such expressions *just* as readily as they learn to use statements about matters of fact; maybe more so.

Do you want to ask why they *should* come to express praise or blame? Why they *should* try to justify themselves or excuse themselves?

With regard to the 'Why should . . .?', compare this sort of thing. You have given me a reason for thinking it is going to rain. This is not a 'conclusive' reason in the sense of a *proof*; but it is a reason for thinking so. Now suppose someone asked, 'Why is *that* a reason for thinking it is going to rain?' Or suppose he asked—maybe in connexion with something more exactly predictable than the weather is—suppose he asked 'Why is the fact that it has always happened in the past a reason for thinking it will happen in the future?' I expect you would look at him. And then you might ask him, 'Well, what do you *call* a reason? What are you looking for?'

We have standards of what is a reason; what is a strong reason, what is not a very strong reason, and so on.

Notice that the relation of reason and belief is not the relation of cause and effect. You do not find out by experiment whether this is a good reason for believing so and so.

It is similar with regard to reasons for actions. The relation of an action to the reason for the action, is not something which is established by experiment. If you have found that he generally can help you when you are feeling ill, then this is a reason for going to ask him for help when you do feel ill; a good reason, too. Now you may say that you have found by experiment that *when* you asked him he *did* know the answer. But you have not found by experiment that this is a reason for asking him the next time. (A very crude consideration: Suppose you have found that you have backed a winner every time you have placed a bet with this particular bookie. This is a reason for . . .)

In more sophisticated cases the disparity between what is a reason—or rather, between the reason for the action and the cause of the action, is even greater.

Now consider once again: '*Why* is that a reason for doing so and so?' 'Why is that his reason for asking him?' 'Why is that a reason for getting married?'

(Incidentally, there is considerable analogy between 'what makes it a good reason' and 'what makes it a sensible question'. If someone asked 'Granting that I ought to try to be more generous, why is this any reason for me to *try* to be more generous?'—you *might* just be pedantic, and ask him why that is a sensible question: why he thinks he is asking anything at all.)

I do not mean that I can never criticize the reasons which a man offers, either for what he believes or for what he does. I may think that what he has given are not reasons at all. But I can do this because I am familiar with ideas or standards of what *are* good reasons. And if you were to ask me why *such* things are good reasons, then I think generally your question would be empty. It would not be connected with any 'system of discourse' or any possible answer.

11

Natural Theology

Those who speak of 'the natural knowledge of God' may
want to emphasize that 'God' is not a term to be taken as
you choose; that it is not just a symbol for what would
satisfy your deepest longings. And here I've no quarrel.

They may say further that you cannot assume that God
is a being you would like; still less, that God likes you. On
these lines people have spoken as though the *power* of God
were the predominant attribute. (As though everyone knows
what 'power' means, alone in its glory.) The infinite power
of God.

This is meant to express humility: the insignificance of
human ideas; the need for men to accept only such divinity
as is made plain to them by the use of natural reason, or
revealed to them in some supernatural way. But when I
hear them speak, it is the voice of arrogance. And I am not
surprised.

If you think that the difference of God from his creatures
is one of power, you will not naturally speak of compassion.
(No more than Ezekiel did.) That God will destroy his
enemies is more important than any idea of God's mercy.
And the conception of the mercy of God is difficult.

If the point is that I am not master of my destiny, and
that no human society is or ever will be—well, all right.
But it does not need theology to show the nonsense of that.
(And the idea of *causa sui* carries much the same absurdities.)
It has no special connexion with religion.

Consider Claudel's: 'Quoi de plus faible et de plus impuissant que Dieu, puisq'Il ne peut rien sans nous?'. (Can you imagine Ezekiel saying 'Pray for me'?).

The whole of creation, everything in creation, is a diminution of God's power. Those who have objected to the idea of God's omnipotence on grounds of this sort, were sound enough. And those others who see an analogy, or more than analogy, between creation and the Passion, would not dispute them.

I grant that you have not understood much of what religion is about unless you try to recognize the disparity between God and man. But 'limitless power' gives no conception of this: you would never guess how religion could mean anything deep to anyone. Religious people have tried to give expression to the 'nothingness' of men before God; perhaps as St. Paul did, when he spoke of the impossibility of fulfilling the law, and the need for grace; and if we had time, there were fuller examples. Living with a deep-going difficulty that remains unanswered can make human life and the world a mystery in a different sense from that in which men speak of the mysteries of the trinity and the incarnation. . . . But then to talk about first causes makes the whole thing shallow.

The fault is in thinking of natural theology as the FOUNDA-TION of the rest of religion, in some way. Here they bring in the whole confusion of metaphysics; whether Aristotelian or some other. Introducing a sense of 'fundamental' which is badly confused.

Natural theology: 'Reason shows that there must be a God'. Some people cannot think of religion except in these terms; except in connexion with these ideas. And obviously there is nothing wrong with this. What is wrong is the attitude of: 'This is so, and we can *prove* it.' The expert talking to the ignorant upstarts.

These theologians speak of 'reason' in a way that confuses me. But suppose they mean, roughly, formal argument; criticism of inconsistences, criticism of non-sequiturs, trying to see what follows from statements made, and so on. This may be important in trying to get clear about religious ideas. But there is nothing in this sort of work which will make a man an *expert*, in the sense in which a man may speak as an expert in a particular branch of mathematics or of experimental physics. The term 'religious expert' *ought* to be a joke, but apparently it is not.

I understand the fear of idolatry. But idolatry is hard to recognize. And a 'rational' proof of the existence of God would be no help. No more than it helps us to understand what 'idolatry' means.

Those who hold to rational theology seem to argue that a man might be brought to a belief in God, and also to a belief in the immortality of the soul, by formal argument alone, even though he had never known anything like an attitude of 'trust in God'. Here I cannot follow them, and I wonder if I understand at all what they are saying.

I feel like repeating what I have said more than once: I do not know any of the great religious teachers who has ever awakened men to religious belief in this way. (When the author of Isaiah, or the author of the book of Job, or the authors of certain of the Psalms were trying to keep the faith of the Jews alive during the exile—did they do anything of the sort? Do you find anything of the sort in the New Testament?)

Suppose you had to explain to someone who had no idea at all of religion or of what a belief in God was. Could you do it in this way?—By proving to him that there must be a first cause—a Something—and that this Something is more powerful (whatever this means) than anything else: so that you would not have been conceived or born at all but for the operation of Something, and Something might wipe out the existence of everything at any time? Would this give him any sense of the wonder and the glory of God? Would he not be justified if he answered, 'What a horrible idea! Like a Frankenstein without limits, so that you cannot escape it. The most ghastly nightmare!' On the other hand if you read to him certain of the passages in the early Isaiah which describe the beauty of the world . . . then I think you might have given him some sense of what religious believers are talking about. I say *some* idea: I am talking of how you might make a beginning.

If my first and chief reason for worshipping God had to be a belief that a super-Frankenstein would blast me to hell if I did not, then I hope I should have the decency to tell this being, who is named Almighty God, to go ahead and blast.

Is the reason for not worshipping the devil instead of God that God is stronger than the devil? God will get you in the end, the devil will not be able to save you from his fury, and then you will be *for* it. 'Think of your future, boy, and don't throw away your chances.' What a creeping and vile sort of thing religion must be.

The difference between the power of God and the power of the devil: it is difficult to understand at all clearly what this difference is (otherwise there might be no idolatry); and yet people with any religion at all will have a lively idea of it, generally. The power of God is a *different* power from the power of the devil. But if you said that God is *more* powerful than the devil—then I should not understand you, because I should not know what sort of measure you used.

If you tried to explain by comparing different physical causes, as you might if you said that one explosion was more powerful than another—meaning that it had more far reaching effects—then I think you would have sidetracked things well and properly. (When Satan said that dominion over this world had been left to him, Jesus did not contradict him.)

I should think that any natural theology which rested on a quantitative comparison between the power of God and the power of physical agents or operations—or: a quantitative comparison between the physical effects of God's power and the physical effects of anything else—would be a pretty unholy sort of thing.

I have not time to answer or discuss other questions

which you asked. I should have liked especially to try to correct what seems to be a misunderstanding of something I may have said. You say that I 'deny that the term "God" stands for any objective reality in the literal sense'. I cannot have said just that, because the phrase 'objective reality' is one which I can almost never understand, and I try to avoid it. I have not denied the reality of God (I can make nothing of the phrase 'in the literal sense': certainly I was not introducing any 'figurative sense'). I have said that if we do speak of the reality of God, this is not like speaking of the reality of the milky way, any more than it is like speaking of the reality of flying saucers. I probably said something like 'God is not an *object*'. And this is a *grammatical* proposition, of course. It is comparable to 'The world is not an object'—and the comparison goes quite a long way. By 'an object' I was thinking first of all of something like a planet or a galaxy or a sound. ('God was in that voice' does not mean 'That voice is what we call "God".') In saying this I was trying to emphasize something of the sense of 'I believe in God', which I think does not mean 'I believe in the existence of . . .', comparable to 'I believe in the existence of a nebula beyond any we have observed': as though the belief were a kind of *conjecture*. And when we speak of *trust* in God, this is not like trusting in some human being in the sense of being convinced that he will not let you down. Such conviction is not even a first approximation to religious faith. I said also that 'I believe in God' is hardly different from 'Thou art God'. Please think of circumstances in which you *would* speak of trust in God.

12

'Where Does the World Come From?'

Why is 'Where does the world come from?' a queer question? Someone asks me 'How did the world come to be?' Now if that meant 'How did things come to be as they are now?' it would not be so queer (though you can think of trouble enough), and we can imagine the sort of thing that might be said in answer, even if one offered only piecemeal answers. But that is not the same as asking 'How did there come to be anything at all?' And I do feel that that is queer.

It is certainly different from 'How did things come to be as they are?'—if only because it is clearly not asking you to tell us about any process or development. And that is also why it is different from 'How did the Earth come to be?'

'How did it come that . . . ?'—what does that mean here? When you ask 'How did there come to be anything at all?' it is not asking about anything in particular. That is one of the important difficulties.

Not, 'How did there come to be *this*, of all things (rather than the sort of thing you would naturally have expected)?'

Nor, of course, is it like 'How did there come to be anything on the table (when you had left it bare)?'

Those are all forms of asking 'How did there come to be this rather than that?' Whereas our question is 'How did there come to be anything, rather than—'—well, rather than what? Please do not get too impatient with this, for I do think it is important.

When Parmenides said that 'You cannot think what is not': well, he was confused if he meant that you cannot make negative statements, or that you cannot believe what is false; and probably, if he meant that you cannot think of empty space—though there is quicksand that way. But he was right in suggesting that there is something queer in trying to think of a bare and absolute nothing, without any relation to anything at all; or in trying to say that there might *be* nothing, in that sense.

When I say '. . . without relation to anything at all', I mean supposing that there might *never* have been anything, for instance.

Then suppose I do not understand what you mean, and I ask if you can explain. Well? And you have to avoid a fallacy of composition, I suppose.

Perhaps you will say it gives you no trouble. All right. But will you not agree that it is at any rate peculiar?

It is not like supposing there were nothing where there is something now.

When I can say of anything that it exists, then I think it makes sense to say 'it might not have existed'. (I know you cannot say that of God—I would not say that God is a thing.)

I think that is equivalent to saying that it has come to be. And that again is equivalent to saying that there are many things.

There is so much to be said here about 'things' and 'existence'. So much that is relevant to 'talking about things' and 'talking about the world', for instance. Well, I will make one arbitrary remark about 'things'.

Do you remember the second hypothesis in Plato's *Parmenides*? Or rather, think of the first and second hypotheses. I suppose one thing Plato is saying is that you can say 'it is' only when you can distinguish between 'it' and 'is'. And I suppose part of what that means is that we should be able to say 'it might not have existed'. We must distinguish between 'being a thing' and 'existing'. (We should have discussed the distinction between a thing and its properties, and there are very important questions that go with that.) Its reality is not just its existence. But . . . what else is it? The distinction between a thing and its existence is obviously not like the distinction between a stick and the water on which it floats; nor even like the distinction between a body and its motion. We can know what it is—what you are talking about—without knowing whether it exists or not. But that does not mean that we could remove it from existence and still keep it the thing it is—or a thing at all. When a thing ceases to exist, it ceases to be a thing. (Not like a body and its motion.) Well why speak of any *difference* between a thing and its existence, then?

If we do, it is just another way of emphasizing that we can say it exists if we can say something else exists.

I think Plato would have agreed with Parmenides, that you cannot say 'there might have been nothing at all'. But he held against Parmenides that you can always say 'it might not have existed'. But there is a difficulty: it may seem as though you must be able to speak of 'what exists' or 'all that exists', and as though you must therefore be able to say that 'all that exists, exists' or perhaps 'reality exists'. And if that has sense, well then by our argument it must have sense to say that 'all that exists' or the totality of existing things might not exist. That had been Parmenides's point.

But Plato's point was that you cannot talk about 'all there is' as one thing, or even as one collection, in the way in which Parmenides may have wanted to talk about 'all reality'. The question of what sort of unity the world has, is one that occupied most of Plato's philosophy. But he held at any rate that the world cannot have the unity of a thing, of which you can sensibly say 'it is'; (nor the unity of a form either). For Plato the world includes more than 'all existing things'. But even that phrase, since it covers what has been and will be, does not stand for a totality or 'one thing' of which we may say that it exists. There are difficulties enough, certainly, but I think Plato showed that Parmenides's difficulty was misconceived. Parmenides was right about 'There is nothing'. But he was wrong in thinking that if you said that 'what there is' might not exist, it would amount to that—amount to finding sense in 'there is nothing'.

So I doubt if there is sense in saying 'the world exists', any more than there would be in saying 'everything exists'.

(And it would not be very different with 'the world has come to be' or 'everything has come to be' (which is all right in one sense, of course, but not when 'everything' is supposed to be a particular collection).)

If everything in this collection has come to be, then you can say that the collection has come to be. But from 'everything has come to be'—or even 'everything in the world has come to be'—it does not follow that the world has come to be.

'Everything' is not a specific class, and it is not a particular collection. Neither is 'the world'.

(I think this raises interesting questions about 'divisions in being' or distinctions among things, as against 'divisions in a species' or 'divisions in a class'; and 'being in the world' as against 'belonging to a class'.)

As regards 'the *origin* of the world'—I need not mention to you that if anyone asks about that as perhaps some one might in astronomy (is that what one would mean by 'dispassionately'?), then it is not clear why we should feel we ought to look for *the* origin at all.

Suppose we are not content to say 'there never was a beginning'. It does not follow that there was just *one* beginning. What is happening round about us here may have begun quite independently of what is happening in the most distant nebula. If things could begin in one place, well they could probably or just as well begin elsewhere too. And if things—tumults like that we live in—have begun at various times, it does not follow that the later must have issued from the earlier: that there are not independent beginnings later on.

Anyway, I cannot see that the idea of a *beginning* of things is so important for religion. Or rather, I cannot see *why* it is. The belief that God is the *source* of the world, and that everything in the world has its reality from God—I can see that that is important. But just for that reason, I wonder whether the beginning depended on God in any other sense than the present does.

(If you say it does, then perhaps you are bringing in the religious conception of the history of the world, and a doctrine of the Fall. And I wonder whether you would call that dispassionate.)

Do I mean that people who ask what brought the world into being are just confused and deluded, then?

No, but I think the sense is different from this quasi physical one.

The question is much more '*Why* is there anything at all? What is the sense of it?'

Or it may be an expression of wonder at the world. ('Isn't it extraordinary that anything at all should exist?') Which easily passes into reverence at the wonder of it—the wonder at there being anything at all. There is gratitude in this too—gratitude for the existence of things.

But now we are away from the kind of question you want to consider.

13

Religion and Language

It seems to me that your chief difficulty is regarding the language of religion and its connexion with religious life. You still seem to want to think of the language of religion as though it were in some way comparable with the language in which one describes matters of fact; and of religious practices as though they were in some way comparable, perhaps, with the practices of physical culture. And therefore, perhaps, when I say that a believer's religion 'makes a difference to his life', you wonder whether it were not conceivable that the same character should come into a man's life even if he had never taken part in religious practices, just as it were conceivable that I should acquire a body like Lionel Strongfort's even if I never practised his (or any other) exercises. As far as anything I have said is concerned, this seems to you—I take it—quite consistent with my position.

And in the same way, you ask whether there might not be the same 'difference' in a man's life, even if he never talked about God.

Perhaps we could put the matter by asking whether the connexion between religious language and religious life is an external one or an internal one. And if it is put like that, I would say it is an internal one. And to your question of whether it 'makes sense to say that a person's life might be different *in that sort of way*' without using any of the language of religion, I would on the whole say 'No, it does not make sense'. But there would have to be qualifications if this were not to be taken wrongly.

(In this connexion questions about the language of religion and questions about religious practices are generally the same, and I shall treat them so. I shall probably speak mostly of the language of religion.)

I wonder if it is hard for you to see that the language one uses should make a deep difference to one's life—so much so that *that kind* of difference would not be conceivable in any other way. I expect you will admit that certain kinds of interests could never have developed apart from language. And this does not mean that language has been an indispensible *aid* in the development of those interests, but that you could not even ask what the interests would be without language. The interest in mathematics is an example. The same goes, I think, for the whole of what we call thinking and rationality—which makes a great enough difference to our lives in all kinds of ways, but *not* so that you can say 'Here is what causes or makes the difference, and there is the difference that it makes'.

Consider the language of religion and the language of love—I mean of the love of man and woman. I would say that there could not be religion without the language of religion, and that *just as little* could there be love without the language of love.

But in the first place I would emphasize that there could not be religion and there could not be love of man and woman unless there were language anyhow; unless, I mean, people used language in their lives—or, to put it the other way round, unless they lived the kind of lives that people live with language. Of course the love of man and woman depends on sexual impulses too. But what we call being in love, in the way that Chaucer's Troilus was or in the way Romeo and Juliet were in love, is nothing we find in animals, and I do not think we can imagine it in animals any more than we can imagine religion in animals. And if we did, we should certainly imagine that the animals could speak. I mean now that if someone falls in love—and if he is broken up by it as Troilus was—then this was possible because he is a human being and because he lives with language in the way in which human beings we know do. Because he can have ideals and plans and longing, for instance, and because he can remember and because he can compare, and because he can have the idea of what life is worth to him. This goes with other things: it goes with the fact that this life of speech and language is a life in which lying and deception are possible too; that is important—important for the whole way of thinking of things and the whole way of judging and longing. Well, it is in these circumstances that what we call specifically the language of love may develop. But I wanted to emphasize first that the love of man and woman depends on language in a more general sense. And I think the same is true of religion.

There are of course differences, just because love does seem to be connected with sexual impulses or with 'glands', and there does not seem to be anything comparable in connexion with religion. But I really think this is much less important than it is pictured to be. And people who have tried to understand love—or explain it—by approaching it from biology have got nowhere; and they generally end by ignoring it. If men come to love women, and if men come to love God, this has to do with the life which they lead and in which they take part.

That applies to much else too, of course—to science, for instance—and it does not tell you what love is or what religion is. But I wanted to emphasize that language is not external to either of them. This may help a little to make intelligible how important language is in what is peculiar to religion, and how important language is in what is peculiar to love, the language of religion and the language of love.

Obviously a man may use the language of love without telling the woman in so many words that he loves her, and without using the word 'love' at all. When Cummings writes

you only will create
(who are so perfectly alive) my shame;
lady through whose profound and fragile lips
the sweet small clumsy feet of April came
into the ragged meadow of my soul

that is the language of love. But you might ask what *that* means: 'that is the language of love'. And in answer one would have to try to say something about the rôle that it plays and, as I should say, the grammar that it has. It is this that determines the meaning or the sense of the language.

Suppose a man does say to a woman 'I love you'. And now suppose someone asks you what that means. What is he saying?

Certainly he is not just recording a fact; it is not like 'I have a book for you', nor even like 'I am thirsty' or 'I feel fine'.

He is not telling her how he feels, if the standard for that is telling the doctor how you feel.

'Well, is he not *telling* her anything, then?' Yes; he is telling her he loves her. But of course you cannot refer to any happening or list of happenings in him and say '*that* is what he was telling her'. In *that* sense he is not telling her anything. (This is what I call a difference in grammar).

If we speak of the *language* of love, this is not because it has a special vocabulary. (It is not as if we had been referring to a *technical* language.) It is because the language is used in a particular way. The sense of his 'I love you' is bound up with so much else in his life now. It is only on that account that it does mean anything. For I repeat, it is not saying that anything has happened, and it is not describing anything. Nor is it the expression of a sensation or feeling. It is the expression of love.

It is here that I feel I want to move to the other point and speak of how the language of love affects and constitutes the character of love. For this is really the same thing. Certainly the language of love is not just something added to the rest of it. There would not be what we call 'being in love' without any relation to that language.

I know that a man may be in love and not show it, either to her or to his friends. But I do not think he could be in love—and here I mean that I do not think it would make sense to say it of him—I do not think he could be in love and never do anything that would rightly be called an expression of it. If he does not show it to his friends, it will appear in his thoughts when he is alone. In the way and in the terms in which he thinks of her; and in the way and in the terms in which he thinks about the world now. None of this would be possible without language; and the lover's thoughts are in the language of love.

Now we said that religion makes a difference to a man's life, and obviously being in love does too. But maybe we should warn against misunderstandings here. It may sometimes be said that religion 'does something to you', or again that love does something to you. All right; but not in the way in which psychoanalysis does something to you, for instance. The point is that the person in love is different; life is different for him, or the whole world is different for him. But in this there is not anything to which you can point and say 'that is the being in love, and this is the difference that it made'; the difference *is* the being in love. Whereas you can consider the psychoanalytic treatment in some distinction from the difference that it made. Perhaps that is why it might be sensible to ask whether the same result *might* not have come without the psychoanalytic treatment. Whereas you cannot ask this about the lover; nor about the religious believer either.

What I have been saying would suggest that you cannot have that 'difference' without the language of love either; though again, I do not mean that the language of love brings about or induces that difference. A man might, in one sense, learn the language of love and never be in love. He might recognize it in others, he might use it in *ratio obliqua*, or he might use it in feigning love himself. But this does not show that the love which is not feigned is something separate from the language of love. And it is still clear, I think, that knowing what that language means is knowing what being in love is. The language does not bring about the 'difference' of being in love, but the language is a part of that difference—I had almost said '*is* that difference', because the language is not the words on paper nor even the reciting of them, the language is the way it is used and the rôle it plays, the language is all it means to him in using it and to her in listening.

('And what *does* it mean to her? What is he telling her? Is he not proposing something definite, or trying to?' Oh Lord.)

I have said this about love because I wanted to show how the relation of language to 'the difference in one's life' may be an internal one, and I think this holds in religion too. Reverence and devotion and exaltation, for instance, would not be what they are without the language of them. But I am not suggesting that religion is like the love of man and woman in any other way. I do not think it is. And the difference will appear in their different uses of language too. But I do not think this affects the point I have just been making.

We may say that children acquire a sort of primitive theology in the stories of the Creation and the Garden of Eden and other stories about God in the book of Genesis, for example. They learn to think about God in these terms and in this way. They generally learn this in connexion with elementary notions of worship and prayer too; and it is important to remember that. The stories of God walking in the garden are not taught them in the same way that stories of King Arthur or the battle of Hastings are. I know you may say that children do not draw much distinction; but there is one all the same, and this is important for the rôle which these stories come to play in later developments or for the way in which they are connected with later developments. The children are not being given primitive ideas of history. Through these stories ideas are being formed, but they are the ideas that enter in worship.

This theology may be altered as the children grow older. It may take on a new form when they become familiar with the Hebrew prophets, for instance. In all this—from the beginning and on through the later changes—they have learned a certain way of using the expression 'God', a way of using the expression 'Creator', a way of using the expressions 'God's will', 'sin against God', 'serving God', 'love of God' and others.

There is nothing corresponding to a theology in the language of love of man and woman. And this is connected with other ways in which religion is different. Someone may say that religion turns from the temporal towards the eternal. And although the notion that 'love is eternal' is important and need not be an empty phrase, still the love of man and woman is not centred on the eternal, on this world's relation to it, as religion may be. To think in that religious way is to have a certain view of human life; I do not think there is any thought about 'the world' apart from that. But that way of thinking belongs with a way of speaking—not just with a vocabulary but to a way of using that vocabulary—and this was learned in what I am calling the 'theology'.

I say that without this theology religious devotion, reverence and religious exaltation would have no sense at all. And yet—once more—I do not mean that this theology, the learning of these ways of speaking, is what has produced religion. If children learn to speak of God through having the Bible read to them, the Bible itself was the outcome of religion before it was the source of it. In general, one might say that theology grows out of religious devotion just as much as the other way about. And no theology is conceivable except in connexion with a religious tradition.

But I said that children learn a theology when they learn how the word 'God' is used—perhaps that he is the 'Lord God of Israel' that he is the 'Creator of Heaven and Earth' and so on—and this may seem to be making theology superficial. Just learning the sorts of things it is correct to say—is that theology? Well, I do not see how theology can be anything else. If I tried to say in any 'material' sense

what God is or what Creation is . . . that would suggest a
kind of investigation to *find out* what God is, and that is
absurd. All that theology can do is to try to indicate, perhaps even with some sort of formal proof, what it is correct
to say, what is the correct way of speaking about God. The
question of 'what God is' could only be answered through
'coming to know God' in worship and in religious life. 'To
know God is to worship him.'

Someone might ask 'Well why have all this theology at
all, then? is it not just so much trellis-work or ornamenta-
tion that could as well be left out?' Well, consider 'To know
God is to worship *him*'. What is worshipping *God*, pre-
cisely? Could you speak of worshipping God—would that
mean anything—without some sort of theology? I suppose
that even primitive religions have a certain lore regarding
what it is correct to say in connexion with their totems.

This question of the identity of God, the question of how
you know whether the word means the same now, or
whether different people mean the same by it, is important.
I said just now that as children grow older they may learn to
speak about God in a way that seems very different from the
things that could be said in the stories of Genesis (that God
walked in the garden, for instance). And you might ask
what it would mean to say that the word God had the same
meaning now as then. This is not the question of how we
can be sure that it really means the same now. It is the
question of what we should be sure of if we *were* sure.
What is 'meaning the same' by the word 'God'?

If one lays emphasis, as you do, on the fact that 'God' is a
substantive, and especially if one goes on, as I think you
might, to say that it is a proper name, then the natural thing
will be to assume that meaning the same by 'God' is
something like meaning the same by 'the sun' or meaning
the same by 'Churchill'. You might even want to use some
such phrase as 'stands *for*' the same. But nothing of that
sort will do here. Questions about 'meaning the same' in
connexion with the names of physical objects are connected
with the kind of criteria to which we may appeal in saying

that this is the same object—'that is the same planet as I saw in the south west last night', 'that is the same car that was standing here this morning'. Supposing someone said 'The word "God" stands for a different object now'. What could that mean? I know what it means to say that 'the Queen' stands for a different person now, and I know what it means to say that St. Mary's Church now is not the St. Mary's Church that was here in So-and-So's day. I know the sort of thing that might be said if I were to question either of these statements. But *nothing* of that sort could be said in connexion with any question about the meaning of 'God'. Consider the way in which we learn the meaning of 'God'. It is not by having someone point and say '*That's* God'. Now this is not a trivial or inessential matter. It hangs together in very important ways with what I call the grammar of the word 'God'. And it is one reason why I do not think it is helpful just to say that the word is a substantive.

Someone might object that we do not learn what 'Red Ridinghood' means by having anyone point either. But the same kind of questions do not arise here. Red Ridinghood is a character in that story, and belongs nowhere else but in that story. If someone were to write quite a different story in which a character was also named 'Red Ridinghood', then it is conceivable someone would ask whether this is the same person as in the fairy tale. I can imagine that that question would not have much sense. But if it did it would be because the question is like asking whether two different stories are both about the same actual person—where we do know fairly definitely what is meant by 'talking about the same person'. We have in mind criteria which are connected directly or indirectly with 'I was talking about *him*' and 'of *course* he's the same man, I was talking about before'. The puzzle about meaning the same by 'God' is not like the query whether two stories are about the same person. The Red Ridinghood example is not parallel, just because that *is* deliberate fiction. And to say that it is fiction is to say that the language is supposed to have the same *kinds* of meanings as the language about everyday things has. But the language about God is not fiction and is not understood as fiction.

(Which is not to say that it is 'true'. My whole point is that it is not language in which the ordinary alternative of 'truth as opposed to fiction' has any application. If it did, then it would be the kind of language applicable to physical objects. 'Truth' has a meaning in connexion with religion, but it is not that.)

How do two people know that they are talking about the same when they speak of God? I know how you and I could know whether we meant the same if we spoke of 'the Guild-hall'. But we cannot decide in that way whether we mean the same in speaking of God. How would the peoples of different races know whether they meant the same or whether they meant something different in speaking of God? Or the members of different sects?

I suppose it would be the rôle which the word played in connexion with the different manifestations of religion and religious belief—in the one race and in the other say. Within a single tradition like that of the Hebrew religion, it can be said that the author of the second half of Isaiah meant the same by 'God' as the author (or authors) of Genesis did, and that St. Paul meant the same by 'God' as both of them, because of the continuity of Hebrew worship and of the kind of worship that was, the importance of such conceptions as 'the God of our fathers', 'the God of Abraham and the God of Jacob', and so on. But for Paul the same God could be worshipped by gentiles who were not the seed of Abraham and Jacob. And if the gentiles worship the same God, then this must appear in what they say about God, in the way they worship and in what it means to them to be creatures and children of God. To ask '*Do* they worship the same God or not?' is to ask about that.

Obviously there is no clear line which divides those who worship the same God from those who do not (or even those who worship God at all from those who do not), and we find that some sects are tolerant of one another and some are not. (I think there are still Scottish Presbyterians who refer to the Roman Catholic Church as 'the Whore of Babylon'.) But the fact that there is no sharp line does not mean that there is no distinction. And the question whether we mean the same by 'God' may be an important one. It is a question of the rôle which our statements about God play in our worship and in our lives. Or, if we are outside religion and discussing it, the reference is still to the use the language has among those who practise it.

You have to consider what 'meaning the same by "God" ' is, when you ask what 'God exists' means. What is being said to exist? If you are talking about an object, then if I and others understand what you are talking about, we can raise the question whether it still exists (whether the palace of Minos still exists or whether it has been destroyed now), or how long it has existed, and so on; even whether it ever has existed. This—the intelligibility of such questions—goes together with a general idea of what we would call finding out whether it exists or not. Suppose I have found out that as a matter of fact the palace of Minos does exist. But I do not think it means anything to say that someone might find out whether in fact God exists.

I know there are those who say that a belief in God may rest on 'the evidence of religious experience'. I think I have some idea of what leads them to speak that way, but I do not want to enter that now. I will say only that I think they are confused in what they make of it. It is not *evidence* for a belief at all. They sometimes talk as though they observed God on these occasions. And this invites the question, 'How do you know it was God?' Frank Buchman answers, 'Well, how do you know red's red?'; and I suppose someone might also say 'Well, how do you know it was your brother you were talking with just now?' But that will not do. I have means of identifying a man, and if anyone doubts my first assumption I can check. I know it is red because I know red when I see it; i.e. because I know what 'red' means, i.e. because I have learned the word by ostensive definition and the rest of the usual method. Nothing of that sort can apply to an 'experience of God'. And the question, 'How do you know it was God?', would *not* mean anything like 'How do you know it was this man as opposed to that or some other?', or 'How do you know it was red and not some other colour?' If it was God, then it was the creator of all there is, it was that in which all things live and move and have their being. The point of the question was to suggest that you cannot have experience of that. I mean that it means nothing; and no extraordinary powers will change that. Nor would it be experience of God without that. Winston Churchill may be Prime Minister and also a company director, but I might come to know him without knowing this. But I could not know God without knowing that he was the Creator and Father of all things. That would be like saying that I might come to know Churchill without knowing that he had face, hands, body, voice or any of the attributes of a human being.

This bears on the question I asked just now: 'What is being said to exist?' We use 'it exists' chiefly in connexion with physical objects, and anyway we use it where we can ask whether it exists or not. This goes with the sense of *finding out* whether it exists. Now the 'it', whatever it is, is something that we could identify in such an investigation— by, for example, the methods by which we commonly identify a particular physical object. We might also confuse it with something else, or mistake something else for it. But in any case, the question *whether* it was the same object would involve those sorts of criteria. But the question whether we mean the same by 'God', I have said, is not a question whether we are referring to the same object. The question whether we are still talking about God now, or whether we are really worshipping God now, cannot be settled by referring to any object. And I do not think it would mean anything to ask 'whether any such object exists'. Nor does it change anything if you say 'being' instead of 'object'.

'God exists' is not a statement of fact. You might say also that it is not in the indicative mood. It is a confession—or expression—of faith. This is recognized in some way when people say that God's existence is 'necessary existence', as opposed to the 'contingency' of what exists as a matter of fact; and when they say that to doubt God's existence is a sin, as opposed to a mistake about the facts.

If you ask, 'Well, when we are talking about God, does our language not *refer* to anything?', then I should want to begin, as I have tried to here, by emphasizing something of the special grammar of this language. Otherwise it is natural to think of the way in which our physical object language may refer to something. The physical object language may not refer to anything either—if someone has made a mistake, for instance, or if the language is confused. And you might think that this is what I meant if I said that the language about God does not refer to anything. Which is obviously not the point. Or you might think that I meant that the language about God was just a sort of beautiful pretence; or perhaps that it was just part of the formality of a ceremony, like after dinner speeches. I do not mean anything of the sort, of course, and if I wanted to avoid *that* I might say that the language about God certainly does refer to something. But then I should want to say something about what it is to 'talk about God', and how different this is from talking about the moon or talking about our new house or talking about the Queen. How different the 'talking about' is, I mean. That is a difference in grammar.

14

Art and Philosophy

It has been said that philosophy is concerned with puzzles
or difficulties. It is often better not to speak of problems,
because if the inquiry is successful the difficulty disappears.
This does not mean that we have found 'the right answer'.
Only, as we see things now there is no difficulty or no
problem; and this is the solution.

That makes it look simple. And some who have spoken
of philosophy in this way have made it superficial—almost
as though the difficulties of philosophy were nothing an
enlightened man would worry long about. It has been said,
and I think rightly, that the difficulties of philosophy have
their roots in language. But it is easy to misunderstand this.
It is hard to see *how* they have their roots in language. And
we cannot begin to see until we have tried to understand the
difficulties themselves. Most 'linguistic confusions' are not
philosophical difficulties, and the attention to them is not
philosophy. Nor is it true to say that the problems of philosophy are problems about how words are used. That would
make them empirical problems, like the problems of a
lexicographer, with right and wrong answers. Anyway, the
man who wishes he could understand what time is, or
wishes he could understand the distinction of matter and
spirit, is not wondering whether words are used in one way
or another. Whatever time is, it is not a word. No doubt a
philosopher will ask him, inter alia, to consider how the word
'time' is used. But that is not what the original difficulty

was. Someone, say a lexicographer, might be puzzled in trying to discover how the word 'time' is used, and this would not be philosophical puzzlement nor a philosophical problem. When a philosopher does ask how the word is used, he is deliberately replacing the philosophical problem by another one. He hopes that if he can bring the man to see more clearly how the word is used, and especially if he can show how different this is from the ways in which certain other words are used, the man may see eventually that there is not much sense in asking 'what time is'. But of course this is not all he does, and a short account like this is misleading. The man who wonders what time is may wonder what such a discussion of the word can have to do with it, and he will suppose that the 'linguistic philosophers' have not seen what the problem is.

'How the word is used' is vague, and if we try to resolve the difficulty by giving a list of various usages we shall not have gone far. It is not so much the different senses of the expression ('time' or 'necessity') or the different ways in which it is sensible to use this expression and others. That comes in. But it is more important to see how this expression belongs to a language at all; how it means anything.

For philosophical difficulties are rooted not so much in 'linguistic confusions' as in confusions about *language*. The principal trouble is not that one word has been confused with another. This will have to be brought out as well. But we cannot resolve the problem by attending to that, or even see what the problem is. We cannot understand the problems of philosophy until we have reflected on language. Not just on how words are used, but on what using words is. There is no single answer to that, and we must learn it by examples or by analogies ('language games'). But these are examples of language, and what they show is something we could never learn from lists of different usages. What they do show may help us to understand what belonging to a language is; what being intelligible is.

Such reflection may help us to understand how it is that language—thinking and speaking and the understanding that there is in life among men—has led men to wonder what things are. A start from ideas of 'linguistic confusions' may issue in philistinism; and generally has.

Defining language would be as idle as defining knowledge or defining truth. But there are examples of language which are illuminating and others which are not. Good examples may help us to understand better what speaking and understanding is, even though there is nothing they all have in common: nothing which 'makes' them all language. There is nothing which makes *this* example language— unless it is its connexion with much else that is language. These connexions are not all the same. But without them we should not think of language as we do, and they are as important as the differences.

If we look only at usages, we cannot understand how it is that language may express ideas.

We cannot understand the central ideas of philosophy— such ideas as reality, truth, things, intelligibility, understanding—we cannot understand the rôle they play in language unless we try to understand what language is. We cannot understand how it is that puzzlement about them and puzzlement about language (about what 'saying something' is, for instance) are so run into one another that we can hardly distinguish them. So that scepticism regarding them is scepticism regarding the reality of discourse.

I

ART AND UNDERSTANDING

There are questions about art which have puzzled philosophers since early times. What is the relation between art and science, for instance, or between art and morality, or between art and understanding altogether? What answers there have been are hard to fathom, generally. We may feel that they teach us less than the questions do. But they spring from preoccupation with a questioning that goes deep. This holds, I imagine, for the view that art and science are both of them expressions of the human spirit. Many writers have said in criticism of this that art is not one single form of activity (or one single form of expression). Not only are the different arts such as painting, sculpture, literature, music and architecture independent of one another, but there is a wide independence between the different forms of literature, the different forms of painting and so on. Apparently, then, a question about the relation of art and understanding can have no meaning. We may study the aims and the standards of the special arts and we may study the ways in which critics of the various arts try to interpret the works of which they write. But if anyone asked what kind of activity art is, the only answer would be to give a range of examples of works which we should all call art.

I agree that we may come to understand what art is in this way. But if we do, it will be because we consider the different arts in their relations to one another as well as in their differences.

Unless we do that, we may suppose that what is important in any art is craftsmanship. And then we could hardly understand how achievement in painting or in music was any different from a superb performance by a trapeze artist. We could hardly distinguish between originality and ingenuity or virtuosity. More important: unless we consider ways in which different arts are related we cannot distinguish between what is trivial and what is serious.

Art is serious in its 'ideas'. A piece of music is written in musical phrases or in music, as a poem is written in language and in poetry. Wittgenstein said in conversation once that Schubert's *Wiegenlied* is clearly deeper than Brahm's *Wiegenlied*, but that it can be deeper only in the whole of our musical language. He would have included in musical language not only the works of recognized composers, but also Volkslieder and the way people sing and play. If anything these are more fundamental, since they give the idiom in which the formal compositions are written, making it possible for the themes of these compositions to have the meaning that they do. Not that any of these themes need be taken from the songs people sing. But they are themes which belong to that language and have meaning in that language.

Poetry depends upon the language of prose and of ordinary speech in a similar way. What is said in poetry cannot be said in ordinary speech, unless it is a bad poem. But it is said, in a rather special sense, in that language. Why is it that one has to be more widely and deeply familiar with a language to understand the poetry written in it than one does to understand everyday prose like newspaper articles? It is not just the 'associations' of the words; it is also the way things are said. You have to know the life to which these remarks and phrases and expressions belong: the force and the importance which they commonly have. I say that the phrases of poetry belong to the same language as ordinary speech (not necessarily that they are *phrases* of ordinary speech). This brings them the depth or the illumination or the forcefulness which they have. 'How can one combination of phrases be deeper than another?' Only because those phrases belong to the language and so to the lives of people that will read them.

But it is not only that either. The quality of a poem or of any line of poetry is something it has in a literature of poetry. It need not be more profound than prose nor more vivid or more graceful either. But it is vivid in a way that poetry can make it and prose cannot. So that you learn from the poem what you could not learn from prose.

What is said in a sonnet (say Drayton's 'Since there's no help, come let us kiss and part') could not be said in another form. But it could not be said at all, unless there were other poems and other sonnets.

It was possible for Drayton to write a great sonnet or a weak one because people were writing and had written poetry. It was possible because there were those differences—the differences between great poetry and weak; in which are rooted the reasons why men write poetry at all. And it was possible, finally, because poetry already had the relation to the rest of language which it did.

I do not mean that a poem cannot be either wonderful or weak except to those who are 'interested in literature'. That would be like saying that you cannot be interested in what the man says unless you have a philological interest in the language he is speaking. But I do say that I should not see the profundity or the forcefulness or the wit of what is said unless I had been familiar with the language for some time. And if I had never seen or heard a poem in my life, then I'd not understand a great poem if you showed it me. Nor would it help me if someone explained that the poem (say a sonnet) is written in iambic pentameters, has fourteen lines with this and this rhyme scheme, and with this special relation between the last six lines and the first eight. I might have got some idea of its acrobatics but I should not understand the poem. I should not even understand the significance or the power of that formal arrangement.

If I see that Schubert's *Wiegenlied* is the deeper, this does not mean that I must be aware of its relation to the rest of music or that I must think of it as belonging to a musical language. Perhaps some knowledge of its relation to other music will help me to appreciate its depth. But if this helps me to understand, it is not *what* I understand. That relation is not what is deep about the song. I do not need to have studied the history of art before I can be alive to the depth and seriousness of the Sistine Chapel.

My point is only that to understand a painting or a poem or a song is to understand its ideas (to grasp it). This means, first of all: to be alive to the difference between serious and trivial; to be alive, for instance, to the difference between a great treatment and a commonplace treatment of the same theme; to recognize how poetry may transform a primitive horror story into a great tragedy (cf. Robinson Jeffers's remarks about the *Medea*)[1] or how music can

---

[1] 'Lately I had occasion to read more attentively the *Medea* of Euripedes, and considering the reverence that cultivated people feel toward Greek tragedy I was a little shocked by what I read. Tragedy has been regarded, ever since Aristotle, as a moral agent, a purifier of the mind and emotions. But the story of *Medea* is about a criminal adventurer and his gun-moll; it is no more

make of 'joy' what it is in the ninth Symphony. If it were simply a matter of craftsmanship or of 'whether he has managed to "bring it off" ', there is no reason why a work of art should have ideas at all, any more than acrobatics does. Nor should we be able to learn anything from it except as we might learn from an acrobatic performance— i.e. learn how that is done and what tremendous skill it needs. We should never understand why people have thought art important.

Ideas developed in painting are not those of music; but generally not cut off from them. Ideas developed in poetry have brought development in music, and vice versa, so that often we cannot understand the one without the other. I doubt if anyone has understood German poetry unless he knew German music; or French poetry without French painting.

Ideas are sometimes harder to grasp than others. I might be alive in a primitive way to the ideas of a work if I said, 'Putting *those* together in that way would never have occurred to me. And it is wonderful'. The Bach recitativos in the introduction to the chorus of the ninth Symphony. The raiment of God in Michaelangelo's Creation of Adam.

I say it is wonderful—not that it is good or skilful or perfect. And it is this difference that makes the problem.

It is like the problem of why men have thought art important. There may be few who have, for most of the lip service is empty. Robinson Jeffers, who is a more serious poet than most, has said that he has 'no sympathy for the view that the world owes a duty to poetry, or any other art. Poetry is not a civilizer, rather the reverse, for great poetry appeals to the most primitive instincts. It is not necessarily a moralizer; it does not necessarily improve one's character;

---

moral than the story of Frankie and Johnny; only more ferocious. And so with the yet higher summits of Greek tragedy, the *Agamemnon* Series and the *Oedipus Rex* ... What makes them noble is the poetry; the poetry, and the beautiful shapes of the plays, and the extreme violence born of extreme passion.' 'Poetry and Survival', *The New York Times Magazine*, January 18, 1953. Re-printed in *Perspectives* Number Nine, London 1954, p. 105.

it does not even teach good manners. It is a beautiful work of nature, like an eagle or a high sunrise. You owe it no duty. If you like it, listen to it; if not, let it alone' (loc. cit.). But the question is how a poem *can* be anything like a sunrise; or how music can. Or why anyone should want to study a Turner painting. What makes it 'like a sunrise' is not that it is a painting *of* a sunrise; for then it would be a poor substitute and it were better to wait for the real thing. And Jeffers would not have said the painting was more like a sunrise than *Hedda Gabler* is.

Consider looking at the Eiffel Tower and looking at Notre Dame (or at the 'Stylon' and at St. Paul's). I may want to look at the Eiffel Tower because it is (or was) a remarkable technical achievement. I might want to look at Notre Dame for the same reason; but if this were all, I should miss a great deal—whereas there is not much in the Eiffel Tower *except* skilful construction.

When the Eiffel Tower was built it showed certain things that could be done in straight girder construction. Engineers could learn something from it and it may have suggested new developments. It illustrated certain principles of engineering. And that is what it is: an important example; it is nothing special in itself. We might call Notre Dame an example of a certain style of architecture. But it does not demonstrate anything—it is not an illustration of anything in that sense. If, as I would say, Notre Dame develops ideas—it does not *illustrate* ideas. If we said there are religious ideas in Notre Dame, this would not be like: you can see engineering ideas in the Eiffel Tower.

Suppose someone asked, 'Couldn't engineering ideas be expressed in art? or are there only certain ideas, like those of religion, that can?' Well, the ideas of religion are not expressed in art in that sense either. Art may be religious. A painting may treat of religious themes, and parts of a cathedral may. But the religious ideas are what the treatment in painting or in sculpture *does* to those themes. The ideas the work of art has are not ideas it received *from* religion. They are ideas it contributes *to* religion. Religion has grown and been deepened by art: think of music especially. There would not have been this art without the religion and there would not have been such ideas without the rest of religion. But art has been a source of ideas, not just something used to illustrate them. This is where any great art differs from the Eiffel Tower. And it is why we do not say that the Eiffel Tower is creative.

We do not find artistic treatment of themes in engineering because there are no such themes; there are no stories. If any art did portray a bridge or a machine or any other structure, there might be ideas in that, but not engineering ideas. The ideas that are in art do not suggest anything that might be applied or tested. A poetic treatment of Samson in Gaza, what the story becomes in this poem, is not something that can be applied elsewhere, although it may suggest and influence later treatments. I cannot discuss this now. I am suggesting only that there can be religious painting because there are religious stories. There can be religious architecture because there are religious dances and religious music. And there are religious stories and dances and music because there is a religious life. In a similar way there are stories and dances belonging to the life of a people or nation. There may be an artistic portrayal of the Panathenaic Festival and this portrayal may contribute to Athenian life. Perhaps there is or will be architecture which contributes to the life of a society concerned predominantly with engineering. Then it will be architecture with ideas, but they will not be ideas for engineering. They will not be like the Eiffel Tower.

Why do I stop when I see an eagle or a sunrise? Why should I think it important?

It is not just that there are different colours and lights over everything. And it is not just an object moving above the trees when I see an eagle. The glow from the steel works is not like a sunrise, and it would not be if it were much more powerful either, like the glare from an explosion. That might be dazzling and unbelievable but we should not compare it to a poem. If the eagle I was watching turned out to be a glider, it would lose its interest. I might still watch from curiosity, but I should not 'listen to it'.

It makes a difference how the scene has come about and grown. I know a little of what an eagle is and how it lives, and it is the soaring eagle that is grand. And the sunrise also: not just the light, but the fact that it *is* a sunrise, that it follows on the night, that it comes with a change in the air and the rest of what belongs to early morning, and with a change in the sea and the hills which night is leaving. The sunrise belongs to nature, it is a work of nature, and so is the eagle's hovering.

A poem belongs to a literature and a language, and a song belongs to music and can be understood. A work of art belongs to a life and to a culture, and it is important or trivial in that way. In the works of nature there is some analogy, though this is limited. It is in nature that a sunrise or an eagle is what it is—that neither is just something nice to look at, as a fireworks display might be.

It is not *because* it belongs to nature that a sunrise is wonderful, any more than it is because it belongs to music that a song is. What comes about in nature may be a dull November afternoon, and if a soaring eagle belongs to nature so does a dead one. I would not stop for most of what is done in music either. But Schubert's songs make something wonderful from the ordinary music that we sing.

I watch because what is here, this that has turned to sunrise now, I have known at other times too, and in other ways; because that is the sky and those are clouds and those are hills: the same sky I have seen in other tones, the clouds that have born differently, and the hills that have the other moods they do. I have known other hills, too, and watched clouds in other places. This is the nature that I know and have known. It is what I have watched and lived in. I may never have been here before, or seen anything quite like it. But there are trees and rocks and rivers and hills, as there are where I have lived. I do not have to wonder what to make of it.

A sunrise is not made of light and sky and clouds and hills, any more than a song is made of notes and phrases, though the reasons here are different. Say 'Put those notes so together and you get this' and you have not said what makes the song what it is. It does not help me to see what this note or that phrase does—why such a slight difference should change the whole character of the song. And this is what makes the difference between a song and a noise.

I cannot really tell you what a song or any other work of art is like. I can describe a sunrise which I saw, and you may imagine what it was like. If I describe a Rubens land-scape painting, there is not much you can do—though of course you can imagine a picture of such and such a scene. One reason is that the detail of a sunrise has not the kind of importance that the detail of a painting has. It would not have made all the difference to the character of the scene if this hill or that cloud had not been just there. For the character of the scene is not the same as the character of a painting; 'character' has not the same sense here. Consider the photograph of a painting and the photograph of a sun-rise—which may be a coloured motion picture. The photo-graph of the sunrise shows you what you might have seen if you had been there. It is a poor substitute, not because it leaves out anything but because you are not there. Whereas the reason why a photograph of a painting is a poor substi-tute is that it may leave out or distort something that is important. A photograph cannot reproduce the sunrise, and there cannot be a reproduction of it, because the sunrise happened in nature. A photograph of this may be a record but not a reproduction of it—not even as nearly as there might be a reproduction of a painting. The sunrise hap-pened out-doors; what it looked like was only part of the story. And it happened just then. I shall see another sunrise but I shall always see it happening just when it does. That is what a sunrise is.

The photograph is a poor substitute because you are not

there. And it is curious that a Cézanne landscape can make you 'see what it is like when you are not there' as a photograph cannot—so that nothing is lost.[1]

Yet the painting itself is for an audience. Not that Cézanne made it for an audience, still less that consideration of the audience influenced the way he painted. But he painted something to be seen. I agree of course that when a poet writes a successful line he is not writing it for anyone or for anything, but simply because it comes to him. A painter is impatient for paints and canvas or paper to get down what has come to him; and so on. Anyway he will not work to satisfy an existing audience but to create an audience through his work. An artist works for an audience without speaking to anyone.

(A love poem may be addressed to a particular person. But the poetry—what makes it the poem it is—does not speak to any one person.)

A sunrise takes place in nature—A poem is written in a language (a song in music, etc.).

I say there is an analogy here, but limited.

A poem is like a sunrise since you can only watch or listen to it. But being in nature does not mean being in a language, and a sunrise does not have ideas. We cannot speak of the form of its development, as we might in art.

And yet what makes me stop before a sunrise is like what makes me stop before a statue or a song. I can see why Jeffers called a poem a work of nature. But not the other way round; nor would he say this. If I called a sunrise a work of art, I'd show no sense of art nor of the sunrise either.

If I say, 'We can learn from works of art', what is the sense of this? Would it not be meaningless to ask what I learn? I have learned from listening to a Mass by Monteverdi and also from Beethoven's Mass in D. Neither can

---

[1] cf. Simone Weil: 'La grande peinture donne cette impression, que Dieu est en contact avec un point de vue sur le monde, avec une perspective, sans que ni le peintre ni l'admirateur du tableau soient là pour trouble le tête-à-tête. D'ou le silence dans la grande peinture' (*Cahiers* II, p. 361.)

give me what the other does, but each shows me something about the Mass. On the other hand I have learned from this Beethoven quartet (say the No. 10 in E flat) and it does not show me about anything.

'A work of art shows me itself.' I suppose the sense of this is: it does not show me something which might be shown in another way.

Do I look on 'saintliness' differently since reading *The Idiot*? Possibly. But I learn less from the book than I should if Muishkin were a more solid figure. Less than I do from the portrayal of Ivan Karamazov; and here I do not try to put what I have learned in general terms: I do not say that from reading about Ivan I have come to a better understanding of this or that human trait. If I understand *King Lear* I have come to see certain horrible deeds, examples of ingratitude and ruthlessness, a character going to pieces— from which I must have turned away if I were there—to see these so that I stay and know I have something to learn from it. It does not show me how I might see any *other* events, the lives of other characters. And that would not be relevant. The drama shows me the force or the sense of these developments here. This is what I want to see again or listen to.

Why should the language and the form in which they come make a difference? (it does not make them less horrible). Is this akin to asking how one combination of tones can be deep and another not?

How can I say I have learned something unless I can explain it and discuss it with you? It seems as if what I have learned must have some generality: I must face other things differently because of it. There is some analogy with this trouble if I say someone has learned from his experience of problems of life. Problems in the fact that I was born when I was and where I was, for example; whether I can look for sense and meaning in my life; questions about responsibility (what is my fault and what is God's); hope or despair. We cannot discuss these as we might discuss questions in medicine or economics. If I am wondering whether to kill myself, another cannot contemplate my problem—even if he also is wondering whether to kill himself. If I understand the problem better than I did, I have learned from my experience of it. But I cannot learn from another's problems in this way. Seeing what he goes through I may learn to take seriously what I used to dismiss as foolish; but this is not what he learns. His understanding has grown or deepened. We may say this also, perhaps more weakly, when he has learned from a work of art. The analogy may help, if only to remind us that we speak in several ways of learning. But it can mislead even more than it helps.

The problems of life which trouble men appear in poetry and other arts. For some, we could not imagine expressing them otherwise. Certain problems, connected with reflexion on death, for instance, may be expressed in music and not elsewhere. But learning from the music is not the same as experiencing or working through these problems. Any more than learning from Donne's religious poems is the same as going through the religious perplexity expressed in them.

Donne probably came to understand his own perplexity through writing the poems. He may show his growing understanding in what he says, the poems he writes. And if I understand the poems, then, apparently, I understand what he shows in them. But I have not the understanding he has gained and expressed there. No more than I've written the poems.

Think of understanding what people do and understanding the portrayal of this. Understanding the life of someone in a story and understanding the life of someone you know.

II

STORIES AND LANGUAGE

Frank O'Conner quotes Flaubert's advice to Maupassant: 'By a single word make me see wherein one cab horse differs from fifty others before and behind it'. And O'Conner goes on: 'Later, Liam O'Flaherty said to me, "If you can describe a hen crossing a road you are a real writer". It never did me the least bit of good, and to this day I couldn't describe a cab horse or a hen.'[1] If he had been giving evidence about a motor accident he could have told the court where the hen was, the direction in which it was moving, etc. But O'Flaherty wanted a description that would make us understand the hen—make us see it as it is. Like the difference between a painting and a diagram; but a painting would not show us what the description shows. We may say that a writer enables us to see things differently. But what he gives us is not vision but speech.

When Goethe was objecting to Newton's theory of colours he said it was absurd to try to discover what colours are by shutting yourself in a dark room with only the light that comes through a pin hole. If you want to know what colours are go out into the fields and look at the sky. Wittgenstein used to say that although as a criticism of Newton's theory of colours this was stupid, Goethe was voicing a strong protest, a protest which was his whole life. For his question was, what is the right word for the blue of this sky? Answer this and you will say what the colour really is; you will have understood what this blue is.

Finding the right word to describe it will show us something about the hen. If I described a fisherman walking down a pier, it would be different. Even if I have never seen this fisherman before and do not know who he is, you would be aware that I was talking about this particular man and you might even wonder what his name was. If I've made you understand the fisherman I must have given something like a story or a hint of one. Like a drawing in a traveller's sketch book, where a posture or a facial expression may speak a whole life. With a hen or a cab horse it is different.

But a story can show us things—perhaps rather as the right word for a hen or a colour does. For example, it may throw new light on things that were said and done by people I have known: it had not occurred to me that those

[1] *The Kenyon Review*, 1962, Volume XXIV, p. 583.

remarks or actions might be read in this way. And this 'seeing them in a new light' is itself a feature of language and understanding language. The story shows me by the way it is told.

I may speak of understanding people I know. But of understanding their lives? Do I try to understand the life of my neighbour Mr. Davies? After his death, possibly. As I might if I were trying to write a biography.

When we think of some life in a novel, going as it does and ending as it does, this belongs to the way we think of that character. It would not be the Anna Karenina we know if her life had gone differently. If someone tries to rewrite the novel with a different ending, he will show how little he has understood. If I am interested in the life my neighbour had, it is always possible I shall learn of events and circumstances I had not suspected—that his life was not at all what I have supposed it was. This cannot happen in my understanding of a life in a novel or play. A critic may speculate on whether this or that had happened in the life of Ophelia. But if he concludes from this that critics who read her character differently have made a mistake, this is not like a mistake about the way my neighbour's life went. The intelligibility which the dramatist or novelist achieves is an intelligibility of construction. The parallel is more with geometry than with explaining something which has happened. (Ibsen's remark when someone asked if it was the pastor who set fire to the barn in *Ghosts:* 'It would be like the beggar'.)

The construction here is not concept formation. A story is not the expression of a rule or a proof. It is a story of individuals. And if it throws light on other things, this is not an 'application' of the story. The force, the humour or the irony of what was said or done—this cannot be expressed in general terms.

When I understand a life in a biography, it is because of the form, the way it is written. A random collection of anecdotes would not be the same. (Contrast what people have found in Plutarch's *Lives* and in Diogenes Laertius.)

On the other hand, I may learn from someone I know, from my friendship with him. I learned from so and so who was my teacher. It was not just the things he taught me and the training he gave. I learned from *him*. And I may want to say 'My education has come more from knowing him than from any schooling'. Here there is no literary form. But if someone is shallow or commonplace I shall not learn from knowing him. No more than I learn from a shallow or commonplace story or play.

Stories may open my eyes to traits in people I know. But if I never saw their depth or shallowness otherwise, then stories would not awaken me to anything.

There is a connexion between such judgments of men and judgments in art. For language is fundamental to both. Art has developed where speech is and not without it. (When I say the frost has made pictures on the window I speak in analogy, for these are not pictures of anything— even though it takes no imagination to see trees and fences in them.) And my sense of the difference between character and mediocrity—which need not agree with my likes and dislikes—rests on language—It were meaningless to speak of it in animals. The idea of 'what he is' comes into questions I ask myself and others, and into my views and attitudes. It goes with remembering and expecting and comparing, and with standards.

If people did not distinguish depth and superficiality, there would not be growth of understanding. None could learn from works of art or from knowing people, except as one learns proficiency or learns to tell one painter's works from another's or gains a knowledge of men and horses. (It is tempting to speak of different 'dimensions' of learning, but this would mislead more than it helps.) It is like this when people feel that distinguishing good art from poor is not very important. For to feel that it *is* important is what is meant by making the distinction at all. This may decline even in those engaged in writing or painting, not just in their audience. So that art becomes mannered and affected.

If people are to distinguish good and bad art, or distinguish genuine and sham, then language must mean something. The language itself must be a source of ideas. And people will speak with a sense of standards expressed in their phrases and construction. For we speak as others have spoken before us. And a sense of language is also a feeling for ways of living that have meant something. This is as true of language as it is of song, or ritual and dance and of art. If people were all the same to one another, if it made no difference what sort of men there are and have been, then speech would be empty and sterile; or a sham, like quoting poetry to impress people.[1]

Or imagine a language that was largely statistics; for men like computers. This would not be a language in which anything made sense; in which there was anything to learn. 'What matters is accuracy and calculation.' And the difference of science and pseudo-science would not be very important. So that people would have no sense of reasons and of questioning. (The pseudo-science which tries to speak where science means nothing. An explanatory hypothesis in reply to 'What is love?')

If there is language at all, if a man can say something

---

[1] cf. Professor Helen Bacon in an exposition of Petronius's *Satyricon*:
'Embedded in the language of a degenerate present is an echo from a world where passions are dignified and noble, a reminder of a way of being which Petronius's characters grasp at, but never achieve. When the witch, whose filthy spells are to help Encolpius regain his manhood, describes her powers in a passage that imitates the witchcraft scene in the fourth book of the "Aeneid" and Ovid's description of Medea in the "Metamorphoses", when Encolpius describes the hovel where she subjects him to her nasty prescriptions as though it were the chaste and frugal cottage of Baucis and Philemon, the reader is torn between the suggestion that the past, unlike the present, had dignity and meaning, and the horrible possibility that the past and present are one; that under the fine language the heroes of epic and mythology were rogues, tramps and sots, like Encolpius and his friends. Something like this the reader feels when Eliot weaves quotations from English and other classics into sordid scenes in London pubs and rented rooms. . . . The past is *really* dead when one is forced to doubt that it ever existed' ('The Sybil in the Bottle', *The Virginia Quarterly Review*, 1958, Vol. 34, p. 266).

then he uses expressions correctly—there is a 'correct' and 'incorrect'—and people know how to take them. 'Rules' are sometimes standards distinguishing speech from gibberish, but also standards in showing that something is better written or worse. Often I understand what someone says although he puts it badly and his language is incorrect. If I know he is *speaking*, this is a great deal. At least he is trying to say something; he has some idea of 'saying' and of what it makes sense to say or ask in this situation. I need not tell him he has jumbled it. He knows that. It could have been said better and it might be worse.

Some idea of this—saying it better or less well—comes with learning to speak. Compare Wittgenstein's 'We learn logic as we learn to speak'. This is an important sense of 'learning'. When a child learns to count, you can ask him to show you what he has learned. But not with learning to speak. And to 'What do we *learn* when we learn to speak?' a list of expressions would be no answer.

Sometimes we've said it better but generally we do not bother. Sometimes we do—a man writing public speeches, perhaps. Now and again he writes an interesting sentence; one that *says* something while the others are flat. A sense of this difference is part of understanding what is said and written. We do not look for it in a list of instructions for installing a hot water system. But a sense of it goes with understanding speech or language, just as much as a sense of jokes and insults does.

It is hard to list examples, because the remark has its force where it is made or written. Perhaps Hume's 'If we believe, that fire warms, or water refreshes, 'tis only because it costs us too much pains to think otherwise'. Or Byron in a letter of October, 1823: 'Of the Greeks, I can't say much good hitherto, and I do not like to speak ill of them, though they do of one another'. Simone Weil: 'Ce n'est pas par la manière dont un homme parle de Dieu, mais par la manière dont il parle des choses terrestres, qu'on peut le mieux discerner si son âme a séjourné dans le feu de l'amour de Dieu'. Or a sentence of Mommsen's that Stumpf quotes:

'Unser Werk lobt keinen Meister und keines Meisters Auge freut sich an ihm; denn es hat keinen Meister, und wir sind alle nur Gesellen'.

It is a sentence to think about; worth remembering. It may help us to see, although there's no question of true or false. 'Talent has a face of its own and is always debatable. Only mediocrity is undebatable'. Sentences that are interesting as *faces* may be interesting. (What makes me pause at certain photographs or portraits?)

Faces may be impressive in a superficial way. And so may 'impressive' sentences. Someone tries hard to say interesting things. Someone without talent tries to write aphorisms.

There is no technique for writing interesting sentences. No more than learning to speak is like developing a skill.

But the way he speaks or writes makes me think about what he is saying and fixes my attention. If the language were turgid and dull it would not be the same conversation: there would not be these responses, starting ideas and growing with them.

The language of a society may decline: not simply with slovenly speech and writing, but a decline in the force and interest of what is said. Or on the other hand, the language of a people may quicken more and more; so that men learn from conversation. If the Athenians ever had conversations like the *Symposium*, this shows something of the spirit of their language—the spirit in which men spoke it.

In his notes on Frazer, Wittgenstein speaks of the impressiveness that the rites of earlier peoples may have for us. 'When Frazer begins by telling the story of the forest-king of Nemi, he does this in a tone which shows that something strange and terrible is happening here. And that is the answer to the question "why is this happening?": Because it is terrible. In other words, what strikes us in these proceedings as terrible, impressive, horrible, tragic, etc., anything but trivial and insignificant, *that* is what gave birth to them. . . . If we place the story of the priest-king of Nemi side by side with the expression "the majesty of death", we see that they are one. The life of the priest-king represents what is meant by that expression.'[1]

It was because of a sense of 'the majesty of death' that the rite itself had to be terrible. Sometimes, unless the symbol itself were sinister, we should not be alive to what was represented. Or the symbol may be joyous: rites and other forms of dances and of poetry. When the language itself, the form or the poetry of it, shows that what it says is 'anything but trivial'.

When I speak so of the rite itself, the symbol itself, the language itself, I do not mean it would always impress in this way, no matter what the life and customs of the people practising it or the circumstances in which they did so. (Suppose the killing were not a rite at all but an assassination.) What Wittgenstein called 'the inner nature' of the rite or festival is given by the other practices in that society, how this one is related to them, the spirit in which it is performed (loc. cit. p. 247). Where the attitude to death was infused with self commiseration and theatrical mourning, the phrase 'the majesty of death' would be empty bombast.

This does not mean that the character of the rite is *nothing* else than its rôle in the practices of this society—as though anything no matter what, could have had this rôle or replaced this symbol. The life of this man and putting him to death might not be the rite of the priest-king of Nemi. But this does not mean that anything else could be the same rite and give the same impression.

The rite, which is a sacrifice, is not a murder and not a disaster.

The story does not report a disaster—or anything else. It does not report what has happened to anyone or direct our cares or fear to anything happening now. We are gripped as we may be by a rite or ceremony. And we 'know what it's about'.

The story does not 'represent' as rites do. We do not

[1] 'Bermerkungen über Frazers *The Golden Bough*', *Synthese*, September 1967, pp. 235, 236.

11—WA *

celebrate it; nor dramas either. (Unless perhaps a Passion Play; the kinship here is important—but so is the difference from Shakespeare's or Ibsen's tragedies.) And yet if we ask why people write and read them—the practice of rites may sometimes hold analogies.

'I learned a great deal from reading that newspaper report.'

'I learned a great deal from reading *The Brothers Karamazov*.'

What I find in the novel makes me want to read it again—but not because I might have missed some detail or got the account wrong. What I find in it comes from the telling. And I could not find this by watching people more closely.

Though stories need not show us anything about what happens, telling and hearing them forms a part of speaking: of being familiar with how things may be seen or spoken of: knowing how to speak of them. For this is not knowing a technique; or not often. It is knowing what to say, knowing what words to use. This depends on luck, not calculation. And it is part of knowing what to make of things.

15

Learning and Understanding

I think psychologists speak of 'trial and error' when they are describing the behaviour of rats in mazes. (Do they always see that the terms have become metaphorical?) The rat makes an error or a false move in trying to find a way to the food. The 'wrong' response may then be replaced by the 'learnt' or 'advantageous' response. Much of *'learning theory' is concerned with the mechanism of this replacement.* (I think they would say 'mechanism'.) The advantageous response is said to be 'reinforced' by 'success' and 'reward'.

The rat does not have to learn to want food. Nor is there any suggestion that in the course of its learning it might come to want something else. It does not learn what it wants. (And we should not understand what was meant by saying that it did—except in a fairy tale where rats speak like men.)

People want different things. There cannot be any *general* method of getting what you want; or general instruction in how to get what you want. On the other hand, Mowrer seems to think there can be a general theory of learning what to do to get what you want. And by 'a theory' of this, I suppose he means a theory of the changes in your 'response mechanism' which go on when we say that you have learned or are learning. He is enthusiastic in claiming that the *same* theory can be made to account for *every* kind of learning. I think this is prejudice, and crude prejudice at that.

Take the simplest point first: that people want different

things; not just that they sometimes want food and sometimes want sleep (as rats do too), but that some men want
things which others do not want at all. Hedonists may try,
as I think Mowrer does, to bring the different wants together as forms of wanting pleasure or happiness. All wants
are 'rewarded' when success brings easing of tension. If we
said that all desires are desires for success, this would show
the same confusion. Whatever you want, you must want to
achieve it, i.e. you want success. Or 'satisfaction'. So the
differences are unimportant. The wants are all forms of the
same want. And all people have the same wants.

By a similar argument, you could show that all bodies
have the same chemical composition.

Mowrer, if I understand him, wants to say that all learning is learning to achieve satisfaction. Otherwise I suppose
the 'Law of Effect' could not be made to work, even in the
modified form in which he formulates it. For one thing, he
has to keep some meaning in the notions of 'reward' and
'reinforcement'.

This seems to me to make his account of learning pretty
fictitious. He is describing a mechanism which he has con-
structed, and which only here and there resembles a human
being. He seems to me to have dodged many of the biggest
questions in connexion with learning.

(I have only his *Learning Theory and the Symbolic Processes* at hand. It seems to me a ragged book, and I have
not found the connexions between certain topics at all.
Some time I should be grateful if you would tell me how
the ideas of 'stimulus—response', 'drive' and 'emotion' are
related in his treatment. He writes as though it ought to be
perfectly plain to the reader, but it is not to this one. I *think*
part of the trouble comes from his shuttling back and forth
between psychology and physiology and talking as though
he were in the same place all the while.)

I have just said that a rat does not have to learn what it
wants. But learning what one wants is a major part of the
growth of understanding in human beings. Coming to
understand better what one wants. Or perhaps more com-

monly, recognizing that this and that are not what one wants, although one thought they were. Socrates used to emphasize this. Much of what he says is difficult (although I think it important), but the account in the *Symposium* of the development of love is fairly straightforward, although it is sketchy and schematic. There is something important in the idea of coming to recognize what it is that you really love, or what your love really is: the way in which your eyes may be opened to what you had not realized; and the way in which this may change your vision not only of the beloved one, but of much else besides.

This is not something which can be described in terms of 'satisfaction of a response'; and I do not think the idea of 'conditioning' alters this. (The 'satisfaction of response' would leave you with the account of love which Aristophanes had given. Where Aristophanes is far above Mowrer is that Aristophanes sees that it is comic: i.e. that it is a degradation from the love which he and his hearers know.) Socrates insists that the development of love comes about not from the success of the lover in finding his objective, but from the beauty under which his search is carried on and grows.

I do not think it is too hard to illustrate what may be meant here. We should never have loved anyone as we have, if we had known no literature or music or other of the arts. It is through the language of love that our feeling or our love has grown: both in what we say and show to those we love, and in what we say to ourselves. The language of love which we have found in the Song of Solomon, in Catullus, in Chaucer's *Troilus and Cresseyde*, in the poems of John Donne and so many others. It is in this way that our love can change our conception of ourselves. So that we see things we were blind to before.

Poetry itself, of course, has been influenced by music and by other arts and by religion. And these all shape our love directly too. (Suppose a young lover thinks Liszt's 'Liebestraum' is the expression of what he feels. And then someone sings Schubert's 'Serenade'. . . .) Just as, on the other hand, art may keep the abandoned lover from breaking up: help him to realize what is lost and what is not. 'L'amant frustré de l'amour pourra tourner enfin autour des corès grecques pour se saisir de ce qui, dans le corps et le visage de la femme, survit a toute dégradation.' (That is Camus in *L'homme révolté*.)[1] I am trying to emphasize that in all this we have not to do with discovering more complex and more all-inclusive ways of satisfying one's responses: of achieving a better economy in one's responses, so that one may avoid frustration, and so on. It is not that one has found a better method of getting what one wants. It is that one's eyes have been opened. And this has been through what has *come* to one, not in the form either of reward or of punishment, but from people and from culture and from teachers. It is because one has *learned from* something, and one would never have grown otherwise.

If anyone says, 'Learning is a matter of achieving greater variety and economy in responses', then I do not see what this clarifies. Apparently it is a physiological theory. But it is like trying to give an account of aesthetic experience without mentioning the picture or the building. We do not know what kind of growth it is.

I doubt if my responses to bad art are less complex than my responses to good art. And yet I learn something from the good art as I do not from the bad—even if to begin with I like the bad art better. If you wish you may call the transfer of my *liking* an example of 'conditioning' (though I should not). But to say that I have come to like the other art, is not what is meant by saying that I learn from it, or by speaking of a growth in understanding. As far as I can see, 'conditioning' would be as good an account of degeneracy as it would of growth—for by 'degeneracy' I do not mean loss of control or break down, but just degenerating taste, moving towards cheapness and vulgarity, and flattening of understanding.

You *cannot* give an account of the emotions that we have or the feelings that we have, simply in terms of 'our

[1] Ed., Lib. Gallimard, p. 317.

responses'. This is what is so fatal about referring to a man or a woman or a child as 'the organism'. So far as I can see, the only reason for using that term is in order to preserve the right to talk about human development and the behaviour of rats in the same terms. I do not say that there are no questions in which you cannot speak of them in the same terms. But when it comes to 'learning theory', as Mowrer writes about it (and I mean *writes* about it), then that terminology is a way of trying to justify pseudo-science and nothing more.

Mowrer hardly ever mentions a teacher, and the word is not in the index of his book. Perhaps this is in line with the tendency to replace teachers by 'teaching machines'. Anyway, in Mowrer's view I take it that the rôle of a teacher is much the same as the rôle of an experimenter. (Otherwise it would be unfair to rats.) He does not mention teaching machines in this book, by the way. But I referred to them, because they would show nothing like the differences between a commonplace person and a person of character. And I cannot find that he thinks such differences important in connexion with learning. Even apart from any relation of teacher and pupil, I learn from knowing a person of character, whereas I do not learn much if anything from knowing a commonplace person. This matter of learning from the people one comes to know, is important. The extent to which you are able to learn in other matters, may depend on it. But I mentioned it here in order to underline the importance which the character of the teacher has. What the pupil learns from him as a man cannot be separated from what he learns from the subject—say arithmetic—which comes through him. He may be able to illuminate the subject; whereas in the hands of a commonplace individual, who knows all the steps, the subject says nothing to the pupils at all. . . . (There is an analogy in the way in which a piece of music may remain uninteresting until you hear it played by a real pianist.)

The good teacher will be more concerned with his presentation of the *subject* than he is with the various

responses of his pupils. His function will be to beget
responses, not to cater to them or 'reward' them. This is the
same point: that in learning there is something to *learn*—
besides methods of responding successfully.

It is through the teacher, generally, that the pupil learns
to see the difference between what is important and what is
rubbish. This again has no place in the 'learning' of animals.
But if it never comes into a child's schooling, he will not
learn much. I do not think it can be won just by learning to
'get the answers right'—even though this would be 'success',
and being told that they were right would be the 'reward'.

What Mowrer says on pp. 236-247 about learning to use
speech and learning mathematics, seems to me confused;
but maybe I have misread him. I have just now been
labouring the point that 'learning' means something different in the kind of case of which I have been speaking, and
in the maze learning of rats. And I do not see what is
gained by trying to force a common 'theory' on them. But I
suggest also that 'problem' is a term with much greater and
more fundamental variety than Mowrer recognizes. This is
especially clear in connexion with the problems of mathematics—although he *still* wants to say that it is the same
sort of thing as he was concerned with before.

For example, what have you learned when you learn a
proof in mathematics? If you start to talk about 'responding
with numerals' or 'responding with geometrical terms', you
tell us nothing at all. A pupil might learn to do that and
never learn any mathematics. Wittgenstein said at one time
'... that the proof belongs to the *meaning* of what is
proved, i.e. determines the meaning. In other words it is
not something which causes us to believe a certain proposition, but something which shows us what we believe—if
one can talk of believing in this case'. This is not like being
given a new experience, as one might in observing the
unexpected result of an experiment, for instance. And if you
say 'they both make a difference to your responses', you are
simply dodging the problem and spreading confusion. The
kind of *illumination* that comes from proof—not showing

you something new, but putting matters in a new light—this is the most important part of the growth of understanding in mathematics. And I do not see how a 'stimulus—response' theory can say anything about it.

In the same manuscript, after discussing what mathematical problems are, and distinguishing them from problems in natural science, Wittgenstein asked, 'Would there not follow from all this the paradox: that there are no difficult problems in mathematics; since what is difficult is not a problem? What follows is, that the 'difficult mathematical problem', i.e. the problem of mathematical research, does not stand to the sum "25 x 25 = ?" in the relation in which, say, a skilled acrobatic performance stands to an ordinary somersault (i.e. not in the relation: very easy to very difficult), but that they are "problems" in different senses of the word'.

I have quoted that because I think something like it could be said in many circumstances. Certainly it is important for the relation of elementary to later education; and also for the relation of animal learning to human learning. What is mistaken and confusing is to think that what we have is a one line development from the simpler to the more complicated, or from the easy to the difficult.

May I try to sum up one point: To seek the solution of a problem is not: seeking to become proficient or competent enough to solve the problem. The problem is not one of how I may attain competence, or of how I may satisfy my desire for knowledge—or any other desire. It is a problem in the *calculus*, in mathematics, in arithmetic. And the question is whether *arithmetic* provides a solution; not whether I can provide one. Until Mowrer and his kind understand this, I do not see how they can pretend to write on learning here, or on what is learned.

And obviously, the fact that other people *say* I have done it right, is not what makes my answer into a solution. It does not show I have answered the question. Though if someone wants to say 'It shows I have responded successfully', I do not mind.

I suspect that Mowrer often confuses (*a*) the problem I have to solve, with (*b*) the problem whether I can solve it.

I think he also confuses (1) an account of the 'mechanism' of learning (i.e. a physiological theory), with (2) an account of what learning is.

I find similar confusions (or I suspect them, anyway) in what Mowrer says about the problems which a man may face in making a decision; and more generally, the problems connected with one's relations to other people. I need not emphasize that 'problem' has a somewhat different sense again here. And in one of his remarks, at least, it looks as though Mowrer were alive to this. On p. 350 he says, 'Commonly we say that an individual learns to *do* this or that. This is inaccurate. The individual learns certain facts and certain emotions and then *decides* "what to do" '. But when I look at what he has been saying just before, and what he says just after this remark, I do not think he has got the difference clear (i.e. the difference between learning to do something and deciding what to do). In the small print quotation from his own earlier article, which he gives on the same page, he still seems to try to treat 'deciding what to do' as a complication of negative feed-back. And he never faces the question of the kind of problem the man is meeting, or what is meant by deciding it.

On the previous page (349) Mowrer says, 'Most, if not all life situations involve some element of conflict; and by means of operations considered in earlier chapters, living organisms [*sic*] consider, compare and integrate these competing inner forces into something called a *decision* (cf. Chapter 8, Section VI) which then and only then eventuates in action'. My chief objection to this is that *he makes decision simply a matter of organizing inner forces*. But there is much else that is bad in it. If I mention one or two points it will be enough.

'Eventuates in action' is an evasive phrase. You might wonder why he does not say 'causes an action', as he might if he were explaining how the mechanism of a clock causes the hands to move. For he began the remark by adopting the language mechanism, and talking about 'competing forces'—even if it was nonsense to talk about 'integrating' them into a decision. But of course, if he had gone *on* just as though he were talking about a mechanism, he could not sensibly have spoken of a decision at all. He might have said that the integrated forces cause the action, just as the integrated mechanism causes the clock's action. But when the competing forces become integrated forces . . . Oh well.

I spoke earlier about his attempt to talk about physiology as though it were psychology, and vice versa. And I said that he dodges problems in this way. He has not begun to ask what a decision is. And as a result he does not consider even the most elementary problems regarding the relation of decisions and bodily movements. *For instance:* suppose I decide to do something; am I making a prediction then?

When Wittgenstein was referring to this question once, he said (as though he were making an announcement): 'In 30 seconds from now I am going to strike this desk three times with my hand'. He struck it three times. 'Now how in *Hell* did I know?' The matter is much more difficult—and much more interesting—than Mowrer's thick soup suggests. (It is connected with questions about the relation of thought and reality; and so of language and reality. About expectation, intention, and so on, and the relation of an expectation to its fulfilment.)

There is a further point, which is also related to that, I think. Mowrer never distinguishes between *causes, motives* and *reasons*.[1] An investigation into causes is different from an investigation into motives. And trying to understand his reasons is different from either.

May I now return to what I called my chief objection: that he makes decision a matter of organizing inner forces. Almost as though *this* were what had to be decided. He writes as though the question of what you have to decide, were unimportant. Just as he writes in other connexions as though you could ignore the question of what is learned. What is the man puzzled *about*, when he is trying to make

[1] Cf. Wittgenstein, *The Blue Book*, p. 15.

a decision? Unless you consider this, you cannot consider its connexion with other problems which he has faced in the past; with problems which other people round about him have to face; or why it is that it has the special importance for him that it does. Neither can you see the kind of difference that it may make if he decides in one way or the other.

Once again, it is 'the organism' that makes everything impossible here. The problems which the man has to face have not arisen from the organism. They may have arisen from difficulties in his family—difficulties of the kind that a dramatist may portray, and that have no analogues in the lives of rats—or they may have arisen from developments in his business, or from movements in the society in which he has got caught up. Anyway, you can never know what they are by studying the mechanism of the nervous system.

And what is important, when you are trying to understand the decision—his reasons, his motives or the 'causes'? His reasons or his motives may each be important, but often in different ways. And about the causes you generally knew nothing at all. In fact I put the word in quotes because Mowrer has not tried to explain what may be meant by 'the cause of a decision'.

A man's understanding may grow with the decisions he makes. But you cannot give an account of this unless you consider the sort of reasons that enter into them. And the talk about 'competing inner forces' befogs the issue.

You have to understand the man's life too. But not in the sense in which an organism has a life.

16

Education and Understanding

When I spoke of scepticism about education in this afternoon's discussion, the speaker evidently thought I meant
'scepticism about the *value* of education'. And the way I
put the question to him—asking whether it would be a
disaster if there were no schooling—did suggest this. In
fact, in much of what I said I was mixing up questions
about the value of education and questions about whether
education is possible. This was partly because from one
angle the question whether education is possible seems silly.
The answer might be that it has been going on for years.
But I suppose the sceptical question might concern its reality, rather as someone might doubt the reality of science,
although science has also been going on for years. Someone
might doubt whether science can really give us a knowledge
of things; and he might not think that the achievements of
engineering were the answer. (I think this is how the question would be put: 'whether science *can* give us knowledge'. The positivist answer would be, 'Well, let's look at
what science *does* give us'. But I do not know that this
would still the sceptical doubts—not at this stage of the
argument, anyway.) Perhaps the sceptic in education would
ask whether the learning of all that is taught in schools has
really made men wiser; or whether it can.

Here, the passage to the question about the *value* of
education slips in easily, because it is natural to follow with:
'Are men any better off with education than they would

have been without it'. I did this, but I ought to have kept free of it.

One might put the question in terms of wisdom, or one might put it in terms of enlightenment, I suppose. Both of these are difficult conceptions, and a philosophy of education might have to discuss them.

Or the sceptic might ask whether in all the schooling one ever *learns* anything. Again the answer might be, 'Of course, one learns reading and writing and arithmetic'. But the sceptic would probably say that this was not what he meant. (And he might be irritated because he could not say what it was he *did* mean.) I imagine that it is because this question *is* so hard to formulate, that some people have *thought* they meant that their schooling was no use to them: that it did not make them able to mend a wagon wheel. Some people really do mean this, but I think that other people are deluding themselves when they fasten on it.

I keep going back to Socrates and the sophists. In one sense he did not dispute that the sophists could teach men things. But in another sense I think he would have said that they had not taught them anything at all. Which Heracleitus might have said too: πολυμαθίη νόον ἔχειν οὐ διδάσκει.

This conception of understanding (νόον ἔχειν) is connected with another important question: whether there is a distinction between education and training. I think Plato would have called it scepticism if you said there is no difference. I am thinking of training first of all in the sense in which you are said to train animals, but then in the sense of training in skills. What is sometimes put over against this is the conception of 'insight' but I do not know whether this would always be part of what was meant by 'understanding' in Heracleitus's sense; perhaps it would. Anyway I think understanding sometimes includes *more* than that.

What do you mean when you say that he has learned something? It is ambiguous, obviously; it may mean any of several things. But I think Plato would have said that there was one sense which is more fundamental. Perhaps the point would be that what you have learned must be your own in some sense: that it cannot mean simply that you have learned what to do when the officer gives the orders. For in this case what you do is hardly even your own action. I suppose this goes with the idea that when you have learned something you ought to be wiser than you were before; it should have made a difference to you; or: you ought to have grown. This need not be so if you have simply learned to carry out orders.

Socrates was trying to get people to reach an understanding which *was* their own. And in doing this he called attention to possible difficulties about the relation of teacher and pupil. These questions—how it is possible for a teacher to get someone to reach an understanding without 'putting it into him'—are again connected with sceptical questions about the possibility of education at all.

On the other hand, this suggestion that when you have understood something it is your own, in a way in which it is not if you are merely repeating it, brings a new crop of difficulties with it. Difficulties which run into questions about responsibility; and also questions about integrity, intellectual probity, and so on. And, further, there are misunderstandings which have led some to think that education ought to try to make people *original*; as if it could not really be your own if it were part of a common heritage and something which others understood as well.

And so on. And to raise these questions, we do not have to start by asking 'What man is'.

Since the speaker thought that I had meant that education of the will were all that could be important, I ought to have made plainer that there are certain subjects which it is important to learn. This was implied in what I did say to Lloyd when I suggested that the subjects which a pupil learns may widen his horizon. I think this is true, but it is connected with the importance which certain subjects have. (I agree with Anderson on this.) And it is a reason for rejecting the devotion to 'projects'—be they on sewage disposal or whatever.

If I say that the study of arithmetic and of history and of literature is important, and also that science is, then I am suggesting something still more special about what the 'understanding' in question would consist in, I suppose. I agree with Anderson that it is a critical treatment of these subjects that is important, and also that there are certain subjects where the critical treatment is more fundamental than it can be in others. But I suspect that this latter point needs to be worked out a great deal more.

I feel a further difficulty, which Anderson did not discuss. Namely: that there are many to whom the cultural heritage in these subjects can never be brought. And it may even do more harm than good to try to bring it to them. Some might complain that Anderson was talking about grammar school education, and that it is foolish to imagine that this can be given to everyone. Anyway, I think there is a question here, and I do not know the answer. If you are giving the 'lower streams' an education of a different sort, then I suppose there is a different set of problems in the one case and in the other. Perhaps one should not try to answer the question what education is in the same way in each case; I do not know. (Simone Weil's essay, 'Sur le bon usage des études scolaires en vue de l'Amour de Dieu'—the English translation is called 'On the right use of school studies', printed in the volume *Waiting On God*—makes very important suggestions, and they may well have a bearing on this question of curriculum (or curricula).)

If one spoke of *positivism* in education, I suppose this would mean that we can speak only of the different forms of education where there are different curricula, and that we may try to analyse and formulate what belongs to the one and what belongs to the other; but that we cannot sensibly ask what the curriculum *ought* to be, any more than we can sensibly try to give an account of education as such. There would be something in such a reminder. But it would seem to me a bit like saying that you are making the term 'language' ambiguous when you speak of different languages.

17

The Study of Philosophy

I

Wittgenstein used to say to me, 'Go the bloody *hard* way';
and he would write this in letters as well. I remember this
more often, perhaps, than any other single remark of his.
He might have added something like (I am not quoting his
words now): 'Otherwise you will never be able to do what
you want to do. There is even something important in
going the hard way: in going *against* the tendency to seek
comfort or stimulus in this or that'. For generally he was
not thinking of different 'ways' which you might follow in
order to get what you were seeking. It was a question of
what you seek.

He was not saying, 'Whatever you seek, you will have to
accept the drudgery on the way to it', or 'if you spare
yourself you will never get there'. As though the drudgery
or the struggle were a special misfortune: and if someone
could invent a machine . . . then we might be spared it.

Unless one understands this, then I do not think one can
understand Wittgenstein's conviction that philosophy is
important. For he did not think that philosophy is important in the way in which therapy is important to the
patient—as though it were simply that there is no other way
to get rid of the evil or the malaise of philosophical perplexity. (If it were like that, then you might say to someone,
'Try tranquillizers first: they might work, and they are
easier.') Philosophy, as he practised it, was 'the bloody hard

way' in the sense of being opposed to looking for consolation or for stimulus. And it was not only a way of thinking and working, but a way of living as well. And the '*hardness*' was really a criterion of the sort of life that was worth while. Perhaps I should add 'for him'.

This is why it would be absurd to look about for something to help you *over* the hard way so that you might enjoy the goal which is really important. 'Important' and 'hard' are inseparable here. (Not because in doing something hard you prove your own capacities, or anything of that sort.)

'I should like to go that way, but it is too difficult for me.'

Answer: Unless you '*like*' the difficulty—unless you see the importance of its being difficult—then you are fooling yourself.

Or we might say: Choose philosophy *because* it is hard—not for the sake of any fruits you may imagine from it.

May I return to Wittgenstein's 'Go the bloody *hard* way'. I have said that for him philosophy was this. And this was not just a personal matter: it was not just the spirit in which he happened to pursue philosophy.

In the manuscript books on which I am working he makes remarks like, 'In logic one cannot by-pass any difficulty. (This method reminds one of trying to catch your thumb.)' I wonder if we might say in the same sense, 'In logic you cannot *dissolve* any difficulty'. (I need not remind you that at this period—1929—he often spoke of 'logic' when he took it to cover the whole of philosophy.)

Or again he said: 'In logic there is no substitute (Surrogat)'.

Part of what he meant (I think) was that in philosophy there are no 'means of transport' by which you can reach your objective. No developments *outside* philosophy, for instance, can make philosophy any easier. Nor are there any developments which will make it possible to reach results which were impossible before. There can be nothing like the service which computers bring to mathematics. But neither can we hope for the development of new and simpler techniques which will enable us to carry out the whole thing much more simply, without having to go through all the trouble which used to beset us before.

Wittgenstein remarks, 'No philosophical problem can be solved by a calculus'.

The philosophical difficulties have to be met and worked through. There is no sort of 'simplification, which will make them any less difficult.

This is connected with the fact that the *point*, or the importance, of a calculus is nothing like the point or the importance of philosophy. Or think of the kind of difficulties (or questions) which we have here: we are concerned with the idea of 'understanding', for instance. And the 'fundamental' character of this notion is one of the reasons why we cannot give a simplified account of it.

Put in another way: If you see the kind of difficulty that is raised in philosophy, you will see why there cannot be a simplified way of meeting it.

This bears on the attitude which may be taken towards philosophy. I suppose someone might say: 'I just want to play tennis; I don't care about playing it well'. But for some reason you cannot say anything like this in philosophy. 'Unless you feel like taking philosophy *seriously*, then leave it alone.' And this means: take the *difficulties* seriously: '... unless you recognize that they *are* difficulties; unless you recognize that they are difficult—unless they make things difficult'.

Contrast: 'There are some rather tortuous difficulties here, but we need not go into these. We just want to get the general idea'. Whatever else that is, it is not philosophy.

Or: 'He has a genuine interest in philosophy, but it is of a more bland and easy-going sort'. Then why does he bother with it at all?

I do not mean that if you cannot do philosophy as *well* as Wittgenstein did—or even that if you cannot have the same measure of seriousness that he had—you should leave it alone. But I do mean that if you want to pursue philosophy as something in which you can take it easy, then you should leave it alone. (Or in other words, if you try to do anything that way, you will not be doing philosophy.)

I think this is the reason for what has been said—by Plato, for instance—about the relation (or contrast) between philosophy and self-indulgence.

Suppose someone said, 'I know you cannot do it really well without going the hard way. But I am going to achieve what I can in it—even though I cannot bring myself to go the hard way'.

I do not find this hard to imagine; *mea culpa*.

And when I do feel like this, I think I have a tendency to be sceptical about 'Go the bloody hard way'. To ask, perhaps, '*Is* it true that you cannot do it without "going the hard way"? Might we not find examples of people who . . .?' And if I ask this, I am in the nonsense of talking about 'the means of getting there'.

As though the necessity of going the hard way were like the need for rigorous training if you are going to be a good runner. People might ask whether there are not examples of men who have been good runners *without* keeping to rigorous training.

Well, this sort of confusion is the work of the devil.

One might well ask—I agree—for an account of what comes under this 'hard way'. For although it has its sense in the way in which the difficulties of philosophy itself are treated, it also has some reference to the way you live. So it had for Plato, anyway, and for Wittgenstein too.

Index